War or Peace?

Also by Tim Hames

The Long Shot: The Inside Story of the Race to Vaccinate Britain (with Dame Kate Bingham)

Governing America: History, Culture, Institutions, Organisation, Policy (with Nicol Rae)

Trump II: Why He Won. What It Means For The World

WAR OR PEACE?

THE UNITED STATES AND CHINA, 2026–2049

TIM HAMES

ONEWORLD

A Oneworld Book

First published by Oneworld Publications Ltd 2026

A CIP record for this title is available from the British Library

ISBN 978-1-83643-273-9
eISBN 978-1-83643-274-6

Typeset by Geethik Technologies
Printed and bound in Great Britain by Clays Ltd, Elcograf S.p.A.

The authorised representative in the EEA is eucomply OÜ,
Pärnu mnt 139b–14, 11317 Tallinn, Estonia
(email: hello@eucompliancepartner.com / phone: +33757690241)

Oneworld Publications Ltd
10 Bloomsbury Street
London WC1B 3SR
England

CONTENTS

For Matilda and Arthur Blair

who will live in the world of 2026–2049
that we create for them

ACKNOWLEDGEMENTS

This is an ambitious, even audacious, volume. It is an effort to exercise influence on what will arguably be the most important subject in the world over the next two decades or so, namely the relationship between the United States and China. I am solely responsible for the credibility of the content contained in these pages.

There are, though, several groups of people whom I would like to thank for their company and thoughts while I have undertaken this venture.

The first is my immediate family. My wife Julia Hames has had to endure me retreating into the thinking and writing zones and hence not being focused on rather more immediate and pressing priorities. The same is true for my stepson Thomas Hardman. His brother Edward and his wife Frances suffered far less. My son George Hames attempted to be philosophical about the whole project. I should also acknowledge Patricia Simmonds, my mother-in-law, Michael Simmonds, my brother-in-law, and his husband Sir Nick Gibb. My own brother Robin Hames and his children Eleanor and Toby are also well worth a mention.

The second group are those who are essentially personal friends. These include Michael Burke and Diane Rochford (and their son Sebastian), Christine and Robert Ironmonger and then via George Hames, Abby Sinclair and Imogen Edwards-Lawrence. In the middle of writing this tome, we also sought to move house, which was a challenging experience to put it mildly, eventually resolved thanks to our friends Mike and Birgitte McLean (who are now our neighbours).

The third category involves those who are both personal friends and professional colleagues. They are led by my co-founders of Acuti Associates, Eileen McGowan, Neil Sherlock CBE and Ian Wright CBE. David Menton of Synova Capital has been very charitable in assisting our commercial activities. I would also like to salute Tim Farazmand at PCB Partners (and through him, Ben Doltis). I have also enjoyed my conversations with Mark Woolhouse at Treble Peak, Anika Randawa Scott and Sarah Clarke at Rewire, Mark Shepherd at Gathr, Ian Merricks from VenturePath and Dan Ilett (a man with many hats). Tom Heylen and Amanda Bibbey of DLA Piper have been kind enough to make encouraging noises about my wider work.

Fourth, there are those within the book trade itself without whom an idea would not have become ink. I owe huge plaudits to my literary agent Andrew Lownie who is also a superstar author in his own right. He was the bridge between myself and the wonderful team at Oneworld Publications, notably my forensic editor Sam Carter, assisted by Rida Vaquas, Hannah Haseloff, Paul Nash, Laura McFarlane, Anne Bihan, Hayley Warnham, Kathleen McCully and Jo Bennett.

Finally, I must single out one individual without whom this book would never have happened. My immense gratitude is due to Ian Armitage, once a private equity partner without peer and now an individual investor and philanthropist. He has been my strongest supporter and sponsor not just for this work but another one before it (*The Long Shot: The Inside Story of the Race to Vaccinate Britain*) which I co-wrote with Dame Kate Bingham in 2022 (which Oneworld also published).

Much of Ian's time today is spent in thinking about his two young grandchildren, Matilda and Arthur Blair. They will live in the world of 2026–2049 that we create for them. It is to these two that this book is dedicated. My firm hope and belief is that it will be a future far brighter than it is currently fashionable to anticipate.

Tim Hames
Frinton-on-Sea, Essex, England

Introduction

WAR OR PEACE?

This is a book about the past, present and future relationship between the United States of America and China. Especially the future.

It is an argument about what the interaction between those two countries could and should be in the coming second quarter of the twenty-first century, set from 2026 (the 250th anniversary of the Declaration of Independence in the United States of America) to 2049 (the centenary of the Chinese Communist Party assuming power in Beijing and the proclamation of the People's Republic of China). It is not a prediction or a premonition. It is, one hopes, a plausible case.

While we will chart the relationship between the United States and China, this book is predominantly about what the United States and its political leadership may think about China and how to respond to this assessment. This is an attempt to make a meaningful and perhaps original contribution. The author does not believe that being, as he is, a British citizen is a liability in taking part in this deliberation. Holding neither American nor Chinese nationality could even be an asset, allowing for a more distant vantage point, with less risk of subconscious assumptions affecting matters.

Besides which, it will not be the United States and China alone that are affected by what the relationship between them might prove to be over the next two-and-a-half decades or so. These nations account for more than 40 per cent of global GDP and are major international actors. Whether what is witnessed is war (of a number of possible forms) or peace (again with a range of orders falling under that term) is of enormous importance to polities and people everywhere. Although much of what might be said and done between the United States and China will be bilateral in its character, there will be very few, if any, disinterested parties. They are both players in the global structure who are too big to ignore. Neither of them is likely to find itself on the sidelines. They will make or break human society writ large. The next quarter-century will be critical.

Why this book? Why this title? Why this timing? Three factors have combined to convince this writer that this is the right moment to make a case that will stand out from the crowd.

The first is that, at the political level, the relationship between the United States and China has manifestly changed during the first quarter of this century, setting the tone for the years ahead. For approximately the first half of the 2001–2026 era, the atmosphere between the two nations was cordial, professional and, bar the occasional mishap (in most instances more the offspring of accident than design), did not suggest that they saw each other as rivals or, worse, enemies.

The prevailing political sentiment under both George W. Bush and Barack Obama (certainly in his first term) was that the US–China relationship did not require much in the way of concerted presidential attention. Although the large US–China trade deficit (from the American perspective) could be awkward, the integration of Beijing into the international economy from 2001 onwards was hailed as a success for all sides. The merits of strategic engagement between the US and China were, by and large, a bright spot of comparative consensus, especially when placed next to the visceral disputes being fought out in the White House, Congress and the two political parties when it came to other aspects of foreign policy. If not an intimate relationship, it was more than an acceptable one. It was reciprocated in China too, even if Taiwan from its perspective was as much a flashpoint as trade deficits could be for a US President. In the 2012 presidential contest, Mitt Romney suggested China shared one key interest with the US: 'a stable world'. This area was not a fault-line in US electoral politics.

This seemingly settled state started to fray towards the end of the second Obama administration and had clearly been disturbed further by the time that President had ended his tenure in the Oval Office. There would be far more friction under his successor, Donald Trump, but the return of a Democrat to the White House in the form of Joe Biden did not lead to a reversion to the ethos of either Clinton or Obama. At times, a deterioration in the dialogue between Washington and Beijing looked like a rupture that might be permanent. Such a dire state of affairs was never quite reached, but the relative understanding of the immediate past was plainly missing. The US and China were moving towards outright rivalry.

What had caused this shift was, on closer inspection, two 'Great Rethinks'. The first unfolded inside the Chinese Communist Party (CCP) once Xi Jinping was fully established as the 'Paramount Leader' in 2012 and 2013. The model that had been initiated by Deng Xiaoping from the late 1970s onwards and carried further forward by his successors thereafter

– one in which the dash for growth was the overwhelming Party and national mission – started to be questioned. The new high command wondered whether it had led to a weakening of the authority of the Chinese Communist Party at the hands of the private sector and other constituencies outside the Party. Furthermore, the growth that had undoubtedly been delivered had not been distributed anything approaching equally, both within the population overall and (especially) across China's many regions. Added to which, doubts were being expressed in senior Party circles as to whether charging towards becoming the country with the largest nominal GDP anywhere, possibly as soon as the mid-2020s, was that attractive. China risked becoming a high-volume, low-value economy which was disturbingly dependent on the technologies of others for its infrastructure. The Paramount Leader was troubled by this. He responded in part by launching the 'Made in China 2025' drive to achieve far more self-sufficiency at home.

This first 'Great Rethink' initiated within Beijing would, once it had been recognised as such in Washington, lead to another 'Great Rethink' in Democratic and (more vigorously) in Republican circles. Until around 2015 it had been assumed that China's drive for economic modernisation would have the secondary effect of increasing the space for something akin to more pluralism, albeit within a structure in which the prime role of the CCP in Chinese life was not up for a vote. It now looked to many within the executive and legislative branches that authoritarianism within China, far from diminishing, was being enhanced. Had strategic engagement made a monster? Identifying and evaluating this changing of the American mind was my first incentive to write.

The second incentive was to identify the extent to which that American intellectual opinion was moving at speed and in the same direction. In sections of the specialist policy communities, atypically, the academic horse seemed to be pulling the political cart away from the old China consensus. This could not be dismissed as a fringe activity, nor did it stem from one side of the spectrum alone. What prompted such a dramatic shift and what does it spell for the future of the United States and China?

The most important individual in this reset was and is Graham Allison of Harvard University. He had been a dominant figure in American foreign policy contemplation since the early 1970s (indeed, Chairman Mao was still resolutely in control of China when Mr Allison first surfaced). The Professor, who has a flair for the popular touch by the standards of his contemporaries, first flagged his concerns in a newspaper article in the *Financial Times* in 2012 (so before Xi Jinping had obtained all the titles that he required to become the Paramount Leader). He asserted that the circling of the navies in the South China Sea which had occurred that year was about more than sea lanes. It was the first indicator that the Thucydides Trap (that an established power and a rising one would almost always come to blows) was emerging. In this reading, the US and China were 'destined for war'.

If there was any additional doubt to be had about the Allison analysis, he put it to bed with the publication of a full-length book. A volume entitled *Destined for War: Can America and China Escape Thucydides's Trap?* did not offer much room for disagreement about the proposition now upon the intellectual agenda. The preface stated bluntly: 'China and the United States are currently on a collision course for war – unless both parties take difficult and painful actions to avert it.' The thesis came with a lengthy series of case studies where similar competition ended in conflict.

A forensic focus on the Thucydides Trap became a major reason for adopting this project.

Third, there was the return of Donald Trump to the Oval Office in January 2025 to contend with. Although the President himself was not as fixated with the notion of China as an existential threat to the United States as many in the Republican Party (including some within the highest ranks of his own team), and more transactional in his attitude towards China (a stance that was cushioned by what he insisted was an exchange with Xi Jinping personally based on mutual respect), there was the danger that an aggressive new campaign on tariffs and trade would undercut US–China ties. This was exactly what appeared to be occurring in the spring of 2025 as Mr Trump first imposed his unilateral tariffs on China and then another set as a centrepiece of his 'Liberation Day' crusade on tariffs, when matters escalated to a whole new level with across-the-board tariffs of 145 per cent on China (which would have seen the two economies become almost entirely disengaged), only for these sanctions to be reduced considerably (but still at historic highs) with an unnerving array of public denouncing, private negotiations and overt brinkmanship on display.

The Trump Effect was the final rationale behind *War or Peace? The US and China, 2026–2049.*

The book is organised as follows. There are three primarily historical chapters to set the scene ('The Oldest Civilisation', 'A (Shining) City on a Hill' and 'The Eagle and the Dragon, 1941–2017'). There then comes a chapter that concentrates on three intellectuals, including the aforementioned Professor Allison, whose works are worthy of special consideration ('Theories, Theses and Traps'). After that, as they will be the most important political individuals in the early years of the coming second quarter-century, Xi Jinping and Donald Trump are examined.

The book then turns to five areas that will shape the United States and China in 2026–2049. These are demography ('The Numbers Game'), economics ('The Apples and Pears Economies'), the military dimension ('Army Dreamers'), China's attempt to increase its global authority via its Belt and Road Initiative ('How to Win Friends and Influence People?') and, finally, what will be described here as the most important 'known unknown' ('Technology – The True Frontier').

The book then moves on to an answer to the 'War or Peace?' question. It does this through chapters on 'China, 2026–2049' and 'The United States, 2026–2049' before setting out a 'Path to Peace', a programme of practical propositions aimed at minimising conflict. This all concludes with 'The Aristotle Answer', an alternative to the much-vaunted Thucydides Trap.

1

THE OLDEST CIVILISATION

The history of China is long and perplexing – on that there would be few dissenters. On almost everything else an argument, or at least a debate, is entirely possible. There is not even a clear consensus as to when we can say Chinese civilisation began. It is therefore impossible to do justice to this subject even in a single lengthy book, never mind an introductory chapter. The best that one can do is identify a few significant factors which might influence how China sees itself and how it regards the world beyond its borders.

It does not help matters that leadership in China has often been a tumultuous affair. In theory, history can be sliced between dynasties – major and minor – and Kings, then later Emperors, in a manner that makes for a relatively neat timeline. In reality, such a division, although it might resemble how Britain or France demarcates the centuries through the Tudors and Stuarts or the Valois and the Bourbons, does not really apply to the history of China. A seemingly continuous dynasty can mask substantial differences within. Many of the most important dynasties have been short in duration, indeed little more than a generation. Others that endured for centuries turn out to be of less consequence than we might expect.

There is also a frequent complexity to succession that does not apply to European countries. The simple direct line from father to eldest son (occasionally a daughter for the likes of Britain, constitutionally disavowed in France) did not necessarily apply in Chinese dynastic politics. Very young children would be placed on the throne, rather than a choice being made between adult alternatives. This allowed scheming relatives, not least Dowager Empresses, to control power from behind the scenes. In other instances, individuals with no bloodline claim whatsoever would simply seize authority by force of arms and then seek to hold on to it as best they could. In fairness, this is less strange in the context of Asian monarchies than would be true in Europe.

Since only an overview can be provided here, four aspects of Chinese history will be highlighted because they seem of most relevance to the world we live in now and expect to be in until the middle of this century. These features are:

- a strong shared sense of China as a continuous civilisation over millennia (popularly referred to as 'Five Thousand Years of Chinese Civilisation');
- profound and persistent insecurity as to where the borders of China as a nation lie;
- the weight attached to the 'One Hundred Years of Humiliation' which lasted from defeat in the First Opium War against Britain to the victory of the CCP in 1949;
- the fundamental importance of the restoration of national sovereignty to the continuing legitimacy of the CCP (despite such disasters as the Great Leap Forward and the Cultural Revolution).

China as a continuous civilisation

There is a universal consensus within China that its defining feature is that it has been a continuous civilisation for at least five thousand years. There is a similar accord that the vast majority of current Chinese citizens, like their forebears, are of one ethnic group, Han Chinese. These constitute more than 90 per cent of the present population, even though outsiders would argue that there are considerable regional variations between these supposedly identical Han, as much as, for example, one could point to striking diversity between all of those who could be described as Caucasian Europeans.

In China, this sense of similarity can be seen everywhere. There are, as an illustration, a mere 100 surnames covering 85 per cent of Chinese citizens, with the three most common – Wang, Li and Zhang – accounting for almost 100 million individuals each. By contrast, it would take more than 60,000 different surnames in the United States to account for a similar proportion of the population. There is an atypically strong sense of what it is to be Chinese. There is nothing quite like it anywhere in Europe or in North America.

It is the core of the sense of a continuous civilisation. How many centuries? Not an easy question to answer. The popular response and that of a historian may differ.

The popular response within China itself is that those alive today are part of a civilisation that stretches back some five thousand years (a few advocates would add another millennium). This is based upon the idea that Chinese civilisation commenced with the 'Yellow Emperor' (Huang Di) who, legend would have it, was born in what would now be called the year 2704 BCE.

Not only that, but there are many Chinese who would insist that they themselves are the direct descendants of the Yellow

Emperor. This would be hard enough to demonstrate in the very best of circumstances. That the Yellow Emperor might well be an outright myth makes the genealogy involved an even more awkward task. Nonetheless, since the early twentieth century, official histories of China have dated its civilisation back to the elusive Emperor. This has been explicitly echoed on a regular basis by the rulers of China regardless of dynasty.

An alternative contender would halve that civilisation's timeline. The critical date becomes that of 221 BCE, with much more historical evidence standing behind it. It was at this moment that King Zheng was able to impose himself as the first Emperor of China at the head of the newly dominant Qin dynasty (and take the title of Qin Shi Huang). The Qin are a classic example of a short dynasty that managed to leave a lasting impact. The first Emperor died after eleven years on the throne, and was immortalised by being buried with the Terracotta Army surrounding him; his successors would be displaced within four years of his demise. They (or more accurately he) created a fragile unity for a time. From here on out, China could be legible to a historian as something resembling a state.

Whether it is 5,000 years or almost 2,500 years old, Chinese civilisation has incredibly deep roots. The legitimacy of Emperors sprang from the concept of the 'Mandate of Heaven'. In Chinese thinking, there was little consideration of how the world might have been created. It was assumed to have always been thus. The role of the Emperor was to maintain the balance between Heaven (essentially whatever happened in the sky) and Earth. Planetary movements and the state of harvests and the weather were indicators as to whether those who occupied the throne were performing their role effectively. This may explain why the turnover of individuals, if not their dynasties, could be dramatic.

The astonishing nature of that civilisation, particularly during its better decades and centuries, put anything that was occurring in Europe to shame by comparison. From Confucius (who died a decade before Socrates was born) onwards, philosophy and thought have been central. Although the writings of Confucius were voluminous, they boil down to the importance of uniting the state under an all-encompassing benign sage ruler of unimpeachable virtue, who would exemplify and encourage upright behaviour. This has remained a powerful theme in national culture.

From these early times, at least two thousand years ago, public administration was essential. China was ruled by subdivision into a version of counties, districts and villages. The smallest unit was that of five families, all mutually responsible for the conduct of each other. Despite the formidable practical challenges involved, there was a form of universal registration of all people from birth to death, centuries before any European kingdom or empire caught up. There were no less than thirteen separate pieces of data to be recorded, including name, place of birth, gender, the number and names of any children, those either too old or too young to work, social ranking (as defined in the official lawbook) and the holdings of assets such as oxen. If Chinese society today seems to outsiders to be somewhat regimented, this is emphatically not the invention of the Communist Party, although its vastly more intrusive system was built on it.

This intense public administration system extended to infrastructure. Almost 1,500 years ago, the country was divided into thirty-six units linked by a 6,800-kilometre road system. There was a set of long walls (including a forerunner of the Great Wall) which totalled 4,000 kilometres. Under the Qin dynasty, an 800-kilometre 'super-highway' linked the capital to military bases in the north where up to 300,000 individuals were stationed. This was a level of sophistication unimaginable in Europe. As early as the seventh century (605–611 CE), a Grand Canal stretching almost 2,500 kilometres was excavated. Be it printing or dynamite, scientific discovery or lengthy sea voyages, the Chinese in the first thousand years after the birth and death of Christ were in a league of their own.

There were also a very large number of them. Estimates of relative population sizes in distant centuries are very hard to make with anything approaching certainty. That is even more the case for assessing the probable GDP during this era (it is still not that forensic a science in the 2020s). The best guess is that for most of the past two thousand years China held at least a sixth and more frequently closer to a third, possibly a shade more, of all the people on Earth within it. The average, very approximately, is that it contained between 20 and 25 per cent of all humanity.

At its strongest, its relative share of economic activity was similar if not greater. Foreign visitors to China marvelled at what they witnessed. This was true well beyond the time when Marco Polo is alleged to have made his travels. In the eighteenth century external observers described China as the most prosperous and best governed location to be found. Adam Smith (who never left Europe) stated in 1776 that 'China is a much richer country than any part of Europe'. Lord Macartney arrived in China in 1793 on a diplomatic mission for King George III with a fleet of ships bearing goods that were supposed to so impress the Emperor and his courtiers that they would rush to agree to a trade treaty, only to find that his offerings were seen as little more than trinkets. There were basically two worlds in 1800 CE: China … and the rest.

China sees itself as different. There is an affinity with ancestors that is not duplicated elsewhere (even Mao and the Cultural Revolution could not break this connection, although the Red Guards often sought to smash it). However, China as a civilisation, as strong as it was, could not by itself overcome a persistent and formidable liability: the insecurity of its borders and how to feed its people.

Profound and persistent insecurity in its borders

China as a civilisation can boast of exceptional continuity. As a country within reliable and secure borders, it is a different story. Partly due to civil conflicts, with numerous aspiring usurpers trying (and sometimes managing, if only temporarily) to seize the title of Emperor, and partly due to invasion by the likes of the Mongols, rarely a century would pass without the territorial integrity of the nation as a whole being undermined. Maps that were accurate in one decade would be works of fiction a short time afterwards. Despite building walls in an attempt to keep out its enemies, China as a country was innately insecure. It had northern and southern heartlands which thought of themselves as a natural unified whole, but there were many occasions when they were forcibly separated. The boundary to the north was usually porous. That to the west was equally unpredictable. There may have been a strong sense of what it was to be Chinese, but exactly where the entity that might be called China was at any one time was far less certain. This created a yearning for stability and for national sovereign unity.

If we take the year 221 BCE and the arrival of the Qin dynasty as the start, then what proportion of that time saw China within secure, stable boundaries? It is a matter of conjecture and opinion but at best it might have been three-quarters of that time and at worst barely half of it, depending on precisely how one defines 'secure, stable boundaries'. One attempt to be totally exact about the whole era between 221 BCE and 2025 CE (2,246 years) suggests that it was unified for 1,143 years, partly unified (whatever that means) for 673 years and disunited (almost always involuntarily) for 470 years. There will never be universal agreement on numbers such as these, but the wider message is plain: China has not been a very comfortable place to defend.

There were, of course, exceptions to this rule when those who then led China were more than capable of expanding their borders. There was spectacular military success during the Song dynasty which, around a thousand years ago, is believed to have had some 1.4 million men in its army, or three times what we believe the Roman Empire had at its disposal at its zenith. But these exceptions again proved the rule. A couple of centuries later the Mongols took China. All that the Song had achieved had been reversed. A form of external occupation was endured (although the Mongols could not administer China without the co-operation of the Han class). Yet when the Qing dynasty was established in the mid-seventeenth century, fortunes changed once more. A hundred years on and elite wealth was of a scale unknown previously, with China responsible for as much as 40 per cent of global GDP, even though only a very modest proportion of those riches were the result of transnational trading.

This reinforced what was in any case – even when the borders of China were quite robust – a central dilemma. China usually had at least 20 per cent of the population of the whole Earth but it had a low percentage of arable land (not much more than 10 per cent of its territory was fertile), it did not have much in the way of forests and it relied on rivers that could be prone to flooding. This remains the case today. Its arable land per capita is less than half that of the international average. China has little more than 0.1 hectares of arable land per head (in the United States, that figure is almost five times higher, and the productive capacity is also much higher). Famine has been a regular occurrence in Chinese history and thus food is a fundamental priority.

There is an interesting comparison here between China and the continental or the contiguous United States (minus Alaska and Hawaii). China is larger (at just under 9.6 million square kilometres, versus just under 8.1 million square kilometres). The continental United States has five times as much fertile land per head and over 5 per cent of the land mass is covered by water (less than 3 per cent for China). The forty-eight states are home to just under 330 million people. China contains just over 1.4 billion.

China then has the advantage of a continuous civilisation and through this an atypically strong sense of collective identity. It also faces the ceaseless challenge of how to rule, feed and protect such a huge percentage of the population of the world in disadvantageous conditions.

The One Hundred Years of Humiliation

All of the difficulties above existed without intervention from beyond the Asian continent. To that extent internal conflicts within what China deemed to be its territory were familiar. What had never been experienced before the 1830s were interventions made by outsiders from further afield, such as Japan, Europe and even North America. China confronted all this over slightly more than a century, hence the 'One Hundred Years of Humiliation'. Without understanding these scars, it is impossible to comprehend China today.

It all started with opium and who would control the supply. The British, now entrenched in India, were determined to rule the roost in China too and the Qing Emperor sought to resist them. It was a one-sided contest. The British triumphed in what would later become known as the First Opium War (1839–1842) and through the Treaty of Nanking in 1842 forced their preferred terms on China. They became capable of operating much as they wished in China and in its waters.

This was bound to trigger a backlash against those thought responsible for a defeat of this scale. What emerged was the Taiping Uprising, lasting from 1850 to 1864. It was a brutal civil slaughter. The estimated number of those who died during this conflict ranges from twenty million people all the way up to forty million, either in combat or through starvation. They were almost all Chinese. There then followed a Second Opium War (1856–1860) as the Emperor sought to claw back previous losses. If anything, the situation was even worse for him and for China at the second time of asking. The Summer Palace was ransacked and burnt before the unavoidable capitulation, forcing the Emperor to sign the Treaty of Tianjin imposed upon him by Britain, Russia, France and the US. Its humiliating terms included the right of all foreign vessels to use the Yangtze River and the opening up of more ports for foreign trade, and it left China to pay indemnities to France and Britain.

The Taiping Uprising intensified in response, with the Emperor largely a spectator to events. As it now constituted a menace to the British themselves, they intervened directly at Ningbo in 1862 and crushed the rebels, with almost all of the land that they had won retaken by 1864. The Qing dynasty survived, but with its moral and political authority shredded. It was also becoming financially dependent on the foreigners who were nominally its opponents. Jardine, Matheson & Company was the most prominent of the external institutions providing loans to the Emperor and his acolytes. The Hong Kong and Shanghai Bank floated the first loan to the Chinese government in London in 1874. The military attention of the British had mostly moved elsewhere (in the form of the 'Scramble for Africa'). This left a void which the Emperor and his entourage were entirely incapable of filling effectively.

So, matters turned from bad to worse. With European forces temporarily distracted, Japan entered China with devastating effect in 1894–1895; once again submission would follow.

The 1895 Treaty of Shimonoseki made those signed with the British look charitable. Korea (traditionally a de facto vassal state for China) was removed from the authority of the Qing. Taiwan was surrendered to the Japanese, as were the Penghu Islands and parts of the Liaodong Peninsula. More trading ports were conceded and a gigantic financial settlement obtained.

China had, in fact, surrendered so much that certain European powers felt obliged to re-enter the race for spoils. Russia, France and Germany joined forces to resist Japan, with the Russians snatching what remained of the Liaodong Peninsula. The British, with a firm foothold in Hong Kong, expanded their territories around Kowloon. China looked ripe for being carved up. This probably constitutes the very lowest moment for China as an autonomous actor in its entire long history. It had lost any meaningful sense of national sovereignty. It had an archaic system of government (indeed the Qing had become so weak as to barely have any ability to lead China). The foreigners made little secret of their lack of interest in the history and values of those whose land they intended to occupy. The Chinese were second-class citizens in their own country.

In this environment, radical action and violence were highly probable. They had a surreal quality to them. The Emperor Guangxu was convinced of the need for political reform, including a major curtailing of his own powers, so as to allow a constitutional monarchy and democracy to follow. A rebellion at court led by the Dowager Empress snuffed that out and rendered him a prisoner. With that option closed off, the 1899–1901 Boxer Rebellion unleashed a wave of slaughter in the Chinese countryside, with Chinese Christians and foreign missionaries as the key targets (although the largest number of victims were those who had converted to Christianity). This prompted no less than eight outside powers (the UK, Germany, France, Russia, Italy, the Austro-Hungarian Empire, Japan and even the United States) to intervene in order to crush the revolt and restore a semblance of order. It was an order that was an open door to anarchy. The credibility of the Qing was busted. By 1912, they would be no more, and a Republic of China would duly replace a dynasty that had lasted for some 268 years.

The new rulers did not have much more authority in their own domain than their predecessors. With the onset of the First World War, most of the European players had moved resources elsewhere. Japan returned to where it had left off twenty years previously. In January 1915, it issued '21 demands' to President Yuan Shikai, which he essentially accepted on 25 May (an action commemorated by National Humiliation Day thereafter). China (which had initially been neutral in the conflict) sought to make amends by entering the Great War on the side of Britain, France and Russia, sending significant numbers of men to assist on both the Western and (while it existed) the Eastern Front. At a minimum, when victory came it was assumed that the German-held territories within China would be restored to China. Woodrow Wilson, the US President, was seen by the Chinese administration and the wider public as their natural ally. They were instead handed over to Japan, diminishing the standing of the fledgling Republic. This triggered student-led demonstrations on 4 May 1919, which blamed this latest humiliation not only on those who were now the notional leadership of China, but on the backward nature of the nation itself, which needed to be infused with democracy and science in order to be revitalised. The Chinese Communist Party would be formed on the back of this movement two years later.

This would result in another almost three decades in which China was not in charge of China. There would be a civil war between the Nationalists and the Communists, which the former was better placed to win until yet another invasion by Japan forced them to respond. Japan went for the coastlines which were where the Nationalists were predominantly based. The smaller Communist army operated from inland and through its fabled Long March wandered across the countryside. By 1949, the Nationalists, exhausted by the contest with the Japanese and with insufficient external assistance, were on the run, and obliged to retreat to the island of Taiwan. On 1 October of that year, in Tiananmen Square, Mao Zedong ushered in the People's Republic.

Enter the Chinese Communist Party

How long the People's Republic would last was a matter for speculation. It had the blessing of the USSR, but Joseph Stalin was not an entirely reliable figure in such matters. It enjoyed some popularity in the countryside where the bulk of the people lived, not least because one of its first moves was land redistribution. Its hold on the cities was less certain. There was a rival regime in Taiwan which the United States would continue to regard as the real government of China (although that thesis would become increasingly ludicrous over time). It risked its standing by taking absolute command over the economy (which had been devastated over the One Hundred Years of Humiliation) and then forced China to endure the Great Leap Forward (arguably the most catastrophic policy failure, rather than natural disaster, in history) with tens of millions starved in a famine. That experiment was eventually terminated but not long afterwards the Cultural Revolution instigated a new form of internal terror. It took until 1978, when Deng Xiaoping finally secured sufficient power, that some kind of economic and political sanity was restored. By then, China had more than 20 per cent of the population of the world but less than 2 per cent of the globe's GDP – this in a country that had been the largest economy in the world for at least a thousand years before the 1850s.

Deng had inherited a mess. At first, he held power in an extremely uneasy arrangement with Hua Guofeng who, while he had been more than content to order the arrest and imprisonment of Madame Mao and the other members of the ultra-Maoist, cultural revolutionary 'Gang of Four', was otherwise disinclined to ask too many difficult questions about the Mao era. Insofar as he had a political philosophy at all, it came down to the 'two whatevers', namely 'Whatever Mao commanded. Whatever Mao taught'. On this basis the old Chairman would rule on after death. There was no chance of reform of any consequence unless Deng could preside alone.

When that moment presented itself, Deng seized it forcefully. The new approach was set out at the Communist Party

Third Plenum in December 1978. It consisted of five essential principles that in their own way were a devastating damnation of the immediate past. The Party was instructed to (i) 'free our minds from ideology'; (ii) promote democracy inside the Party and the legal system; (iii) review the past to guide the future; (iv) curb excessive bureaucracy; and (v) allow some regions and enterprises to get rich first. To many this might seem like a set of statements of the obvious. There were still plenty inside the Party who remained loyal to the memory of Mao for whom this was (counter-)revolutionary material. It went well beyond reversing the Cultural Revolution. It suggested an entirely new (even quasi-capitalist) path should be undertaken.

For Deng, it was economic renewal or nothing. It would not be long before he made it an official target to quadruple the GDP of China by the year 2000, a campaign that would necessitate a growth rate of around 7 per cent each year to be realised. This struck many as wildly ambitious.

The reality was that China was a basket case. In 1978, it had an estimated per capita GDP of $156, which meant it ranked 172nd on the planet. It was an agricultural society which managed to combine rising life expectancy and very respectable literacy rates with abnormal poverty. Bicycles and radios were considered luxuries beyond the means of most of its citizens. The authorities set prices for 97 per cent of all products. There was only one domestic bank (the People's Bank of China), although there was so little money about, one may have been enough. Its trade accounted for less than 1 per cent of all global transactions. Its bureaucracy had been utterly undermined by the decision under the Cultural Revolution to scale back higher education and end competitive examinations, a merit-based approach that China had introduced many centuries before any nation in Europe. By rights, the end of Mao should have been the cause of national celebration, and his reputation should have been the blackest of spots on what was his Party. Surely, he was ripe for repudiation.

Yet the legacy and legitimacy of both Mao himself and the Chinese Communist Party rested on the Party having restored (bar Taiwan) the unity of China and (bar a degree of dependence on the USSR in the 1950s) its independence. To an extent that most outsiders do not appreciate, this remains its political calling card. It has done what no other force could do in more than a century. It meant that even at the very height of his power, Deng could never explicitly assail Mao or deliver the equivalent of Nikita Khrushchev's 1956 secret speech condemning Stalin's regime.

This is the China that the United States and Europe will be dealing with in the 2026 to 2049 era. It is one where the shared sense of being the oldest continuous civilisation is utterly central. It is one which has long faced the challenge of defending its borders and feeding its population. It is one where a century of national humiliation casts an enormous shadow over how it views the outside world. It is one where the Communist Party's claim to continued legitimacy is that it is the sole reliable guarantor of a unity and an independence that could still be imperilled.

This remains the strongest card held by the Communist Party and it is not one to be treated lightly. Fear of malign foreign intervention in China's affairs is rarely far below the surface, nor is the sense that outsiders, including those from the United States, lack respect for China not only as a country but as a civilisation. From time to time incidents arise that allow this sentiment to erupt to an extent that the authorities in Beijing find themselves having to restrain the public. One such case was the accidental bombing of the Chinese Embassy in

Belgrade, Serbia during the Kosovo conflict in 1999, which left five dead and obliged President Clinton to apologise. It does not take much to light the blue touchpaper. It does not need official sanction for a flame to take hold.

There is, though, a potential paradox worthy of note over the second quarter of this century. The more consequential that China becomes as an economic and political actor in the world, then the less tangible is the claim that only the Communist Party can ensure that it does not lapse into the lamentable conditions of the past. Instability is a continuing concern, but the legitimacy of one-party rule requires more than that to ensure its viability. The oldest of civilisations might now be able to survive and thrive as a quite different sort of China.

2

A (SHINING) CITY ON A HILL

All nations think that they are different. That is inevitable. What would be the point of being an autonomous nation if that entity were, to all intents and purposes, indistinguishable from one or many others? And so, they brand themselves with individual flags, engage in legal battles to protect 'their' foods, and boast about their cultural heritage and storied forefathers. To that extent neither the United States nor China is unique. That they see themselves as different is not a necessary source of bilateral friction.

The intriguing aspect of the United States and China, however, is that they regard themselves as fundamentally different from the norm, each an outlier, and to a degree an example to others. This is not systemic, in the sense that the US and the USSR stood for diametrically opposed visions and views of human society. It is instead explained by the extent to which history (supplemented by geography) has led, even compelled, the United States and China to look at the outside world in a different way to others in Europe, Asia, Africa, the rest of the Americas and Oceania. For China, the core argument is that it is less a country as such than a custodian of the oldest continuous civilisation to be found anywhere on Earth. That first principle has then been conditioned by a very long period in which its borders were profoundly and persistently insecure, the One Hundred Years of Humiliation it endured, and the arrival of the Communist Party on the scene in 1949. If you do not appreciate these factors, you do not understand China. They are what make modern China what it is and largely explain what its foreign policy will be.

On the other hand, the United States makes its own claim for its status as an exception. Its defining argument is that it is less a country than an idea or an ideal. What this idea is, and whether it can be pursued through US foreign policy, has been the subject of bitter debate since at least 1776. This principle has been conditioned by a far shorter history but one in which its borders have not only been secure but have expanded very dramatically, an 'American Century' during which its status as a superpower from 1945 onwards has been of transformational consequence. At no stage, however, has this led to anything like a universal consensus on what the role of the nation in the wider world should be.

The only 'ism'

Ronald Reagan, the most articulate President of recent memory, was fond of describing the United States as a 'shining city on a hill'. His farewell address as President concluded with his personal exposition as to what this meant to him. He acknowledged that the origin of the phrase belonged to John Winthrop, a prominent pilgrim, who used the term in a sermon in 1630 (he referred to 'a city on a hill' – Mr Reagan added the 'shining' element to it). That sermon was actually delivered in

Southampton, England, not anywhere near what we would now call the United States, in front of an aspiring band of would-be Massachusetts Bay colonists, before they boarded their vessel *Arbella* for the perilous voyage to found what would become Boston. No one assembled knew what their hoped-for new homeland looked like. Winthrop quoted Matthew 5.14 in which Jesus asserts that 'a city on a hill cannot be hid'. This is a statement that is capable of multiple interpretations. It could be inspiring or issued as closer to a warning. Was the (shining) city there to be defended against hostile forces, or to be admired and emulated?

So there are two camps (and Reagan was plainly in the second). Within those two broad segments there are important categories. The history of the United States and its approach and attitude to the outside world is at one level (although somewhat superficially) a competition between two visions, but at another level rather more complicated than that.

This is the background to the argument about what exactly 'Americanism' is. There are three aspects to this worthy of note. They apply regardless of whether those involved are secular or religious in orientation. The first is that there is such a concept of 'Americanism' and it has neither disappeared nor become diluted as other nation-states have been established over time. It is encapsulated in the words of the eminent American historian Richard Hofstadter: 'it has been our fate as a nation not to have ideologies, but to be one.' He himself had been a (rather reluctant) Communist in his youth, although he would abandon that stance in later life, and his words were certainly not written out of a sense of identification with an Almighty. Liberals as well as conservatives do not merely accept but embrace the thesis that there is 'Americanism' in a manner that would make no sense if one attempted to make the case for a 'Britishism' or a

'Frenchism', let alone a 'Chineseism', and that 'Americanism' should shape US thinking.

The second element is that 'Americanism' is a gift that has been bestowed upon the nation. Those of a religious disposition would credit God for the gift. Others (including some who also have deep faith) would credit the extraordinary talents of those who declared independence from Great Britain and then framed the US Constitution not long afterwards. Whatever the source, 'Americanism' is something that the United States has acquired either because it was especially deserving of it, or through some divine or other form of immense benign fortune.

Finally, whatever the components of 'Americanism' might be – the most widely recognised set would include republicanism, freedom, liberty, constitutionalism, universal rights and the rule of law – these national values are what set the United States apart in the international arena.

Yet what to do with them? To simplify outrageously (and then correct for complexity thereafter), let us assert that there are two views here, the 'monastic' and then the 'missionary'.

The 'monastic' approach holds that Americanism is precious, yet fragile. It has to be preserved and defended. It was not designed for or delivered to anyone else other than the United States. It is not a product for export. Indeed, there is the risk that if Americans were to emerge from the 'city on a hill' and offer up Americanism for external consumption, it would be attacked, corrupted or rejected. Americanism can be maintained only by a form of voluntary quarantine.

The 'missionary' attitude is the polar opposite. It is that Americanism should be available to all humankind, without much amendment or adaptation, as a matter of moral imperative. Samuel Huntington, a scholar to rival Richard Hofstadter but working largely later, saw the United States as a 'missionary nation', which should be unapologetic about the superiority of its system and wish to see it accepted as such (and adopted) whether elites in other countries were enthusiastic about this or not. He contended that 'non-western people should commit themselves to the western values of democracy, free markets, rule of law and should embody these values in their institutions'. For 'western' in this sense, read American and Americanism.

This is a sweeping division but one that does not lack credibility or legitimacy. It has had the potential side-effect of suggesting that the United States has in its history either held to a 'monastic' approach (isolationism) or to a 'missionary' one (internationalism). At the most extreme, it has been posited that the United States was essentially monastic/isolationist from 1776 to 1941 (with a blip in 1917–1918) and then missionary/internationalist after that point.

This is far, far too simplistic. There has always been an argument about the role of the United States in the world. There has never been an absolute consensus in favour of one of two visions rather than the other. The disagreements on this have been central to the various party systems that have emerged in the course of the past 250 years and to intra-party disputes within them. It would be more accurate to think of (comparative) isolationism as consisting of three strands: idealist isolationism, regional isolationism and selective isolationism, and of internationalism as being similarly considered as a contest between nationalist internationalism, idealistic (liberal) internationalism and idealistic (conservative) internationalism, with the divide between the last two categories reflecting domestic political priorities as much as foreign policy themes.

This requires more of a kaleidoscope mentality than the binary formula but it captures the more subtle variations in the approach of the United States to the outside world and better fits the agendas and instincts of Presidents who have been especially significant in this field, be they George Washington (an idealistic isolationist, largely), Thomas Jefferson (selective isolationist), James Monroe (regional isolationist), Theodore Roosevelt (nationalist internationalist), Woodrow Wilson (idealistic liberal internationalist) and Mr Reagan (idealistic conservative internationalist). Most Presidents (Richard Nixon is a conceivable deviation) can be placed, with greater or lesser intensity depending on their tenure in office and level of personal engagement in foreign affairs, into one of these six boxes. Whether that still holds true now is a vital question.

Taking this as a starting point, the history of American foreign policy up until Pearl Harbor and entry into the Second World War, in a far more absolute sense than the First World War, can be seen as follows.

The War of Independence was an uprising by the colonies against the British. Those who fought for the colonies included those for whom the very principle of being British subjects was an affront, and others who felt obliged to rebel less out of innate principle than because the policies Britain was pursuing at that time were unacceptable to their ideals and interests. A more adroit and astute monarch and Parliament in London might have maintained their loyalties. For many of them, abandoning what was seen as a mother country was painful.

The War was fought and won by the colonialists on their own soil and essentially by their own hand. The fledgling United States was aided and abetted by a de facto alliance with France (with Spain and the Netherlands assisting in more minor respects). The assistance of the *ancien régime* in France was certainly not motivated by empathy with the stirring language of the Declaration of Independence (quite the opposite); it was an opportunistic intervention designed to inconvenience Britain as part of its wider struggle with France for political mastery. This blew hot and cold in terms of direct conflict but was continuous in indirect activities. The emergence of an autonomous United States in North America was, nonetheless, regarded as a tactical triumph for France. After all, the war ended with the 1783 Treaty of Paris, signed in a hotel on the left bank of the Seine.

The first foreign policy divide was thus not between isolationists and internationalists (there was no one agitating for the new United States to throw what weight it had around elsewhere) but among what could be termed the selective isolationists. Did the new United States deem Britain or France to be the larger menace towards it? This became extremely relevant when outright war broke out between Britain and France in 1793 following the French Revolution, which prompted the United States to pass the Neutrality Act of 1794 with the initial aspiration of steering clear of hostilities. This line would prove hard to hold and a stark split emerged between the Federalists (such as Alexander Hamilton, the first Secretary of the Treasury) whose empathies were with the British, and the Republicans or Democratic-Republicans (led by Thomas Jefferson, the first Secretary of State) whose sympathies tended towards France. There was a bitter battle over the Jay Treaty ratified in 1795 (backed by Hamilton) which was seen as assisting Britain. There would be a further dispute once John Adams had become the President over the Foreign Intercourse Bill of 1798, which sought to stipulate the size and role of an American diplomatic presence overseas. Once again this was highly partisan.

This is an era that is perhaps characterised as something closer to absolute isolationism: predominantly because George Washington himself, as the first President, stood above the fray when it came to alignment even of the softest form with either Britain or France. In his farewell address as President, he warned against becoming ensnared in alliances and observed that 'Europe has a set of primary interests, which to us have none or a very remote relation'. This has been deemed by many historians to be a statement of isolationism. It was more of a plea for it. The bulk of this lengthy (written) address was actually a doomed decrial of party factionalism.

When Thomas Jefferson became President in 1801, American foreign policy switched in focus. He was hardly an internationalist of any hue but within selective isolationism he definitely saw Britain as a larger threat to his notion of the United States as an 'empire of liberty'. The rise of Napoleon in France (scarcely an Emperor of Liberty) threw a spanner in the works and limited the extent to which his instinctive alignment with Paris could be translated into assistance. The Embargo Act of 1807 forbade US trade with either Britain or France, to avoid any perception of taking one side or the other. The overall sense of US policy was, though, that if in the last decade of the eighteenth century it was strictly speaking non-aligned (but leaned towards Britain), in the first decade of the nineteenth century it was also non-aligned (but leaned towards France). This would become even clearer under the next President, James Madison (as we will see).

By the 1820s, the primary source of concern for the United States within what can continue to be dubbed selective isolationism was not Britain, nor France, but Spain. After a decade-long war of independence, Mexico broke free from Spanish rule in 1821, and Guatemala, Honduras, El Salvador, Nicaragua and Costa Rica followed by 1823. There was the serious danger that the independent nations emerging where Madrid had once reigned supreme would be considered enticing acquisitions by Britain and France. It was not in the national interests of the United States to witness a scramble for the Americas. This required a pivot from selective isolationism to regional isolationism with the Monroe Doctrine of 1823. This was a statement of intent as to how the US would assert itself in what it saw as its own backyard. It held that the United States would oppose any foreign interference in any part of the Americas.

Exactly how this position could be enforced, given that the US was a minor military force, was an unanswered question. Nevertheless, it has remained a central doctrine of US foreign policy for more than two hundred years. It is hardly likely to be repudiated at any moment in the future.

It also signalled that slowly but surely the United States was being obliged to edge away from what had been selective isolationism towards something closer to selective internationalism (but with enduring partisan disagreement as to what specifically this should entail). In its internal politics, the nation was becoming increasingly divided by the slavery question, which reflected not merely an ethical dispute but also an economic one. The states of the North were becoming increasingly mercantile (and more industrial) in their outlook, while those of the South remained firmly agricultural with the export of cotton a key interest. Domestic dissensus was destined to be reflected in how America saw the outside world.

An illuminating if obscure illustration of this change was the Clayton–Bulwer Treaty of 1850. More than five decades before the construction of the Panama Canal was completed, the US had become interested in finding a crossing between the Pacific and the Atlantic in Nicaragua. This had the potential to create a conflict between American and British economic interests. In the past, this may have been the catalyst for political hostility, but in the 1850s it inspired diplomacy.

The treaty was a tacit recognition by Britain of the Monroe Doctrine and rising US authority. The provisions of this Anglo-American agreement were that neither country would build a canal without the consent and co-operation of the other, neither would fortify nor found additional colonies in the region and if/when a canal was built, both parties would ensure that access to it would be made available on the same commercial terms to all shipping. As it happened, for a combination of tactical and technical reasons, no canal in Nicaragua ever emerged. The fact that the United States contemplated one hardly suggested a truly isolationist foreign policy.

Introspection was about to trump both isolationism and internationalism (selective or not). The role of the United States in international affairs in a political sense was not an explicit aspect of the Civil War. There was a substantial element to the dispute which did relate to economics and with it, by extension, free trade versus tariffs and the ambitions that the US had for itself.

The Civil War was a potential opportunity for the main European powers, Britain and France. Although the emotional or moral appeal of the Union was compelling (particularly after Abraham Lincoln had issued the Emancipation Proclamation), the economic interests of the British Empire (and to a lesser extent that of France) lay with the Confederacy and with free trade. Moreover, if the United States were to be split into two nations, it would be in a considerably weaker position to resist imperialist endeavours within the Americas. Hence, both Britain and France considered recognising the Confederacy as a legitimate separate nation. Ultimately, however, they opted to wait it out and assess the landscape once the war ended.

Events during and after it nudged the United States back towards selective isolationism. The United States entered a period of introspection. Finding a new settlement for the restored nation (including Reconstruction in the South until largely abandoned in terms of civil rights from 1877) mattered much more than reaching an agreement on how the country would engage with other nations.

That it switched again was almost accidental. A series of blunders by Spain surrounding its management of Cuba in the 1890s led to a much larger showdown with the United States than was necessary. It was a battle for which the authorities in Madrid were spectacularly poorly prepared. It was a total rout. Somehow a dispute over a sizeable but hardly vast island in the Caribbean led Spain to a humiliating defeat in a matter of months in 1898, not only losing control of Cuba but ceding Puerto Rico, Guam and the Philippines to the US too, as well as controlling influence over what had been until recently called the Kingdom of Hawaii.

This had not really been the masterplan of the then President, William McKinley. His objectives were not imperialist but rather more pacific in their character (he was mentioned approvingly by Donald Trump as an enlightened peacemaker in his 2025 Inaugural Address). If he stumbled into something approaching an outright nationalist internationalism (a first for the United States), then his second Vice President and successor after his assassination in 1901, Theodore Roosevelt, drove it forward. It was this President who started to build up the American fleet, stared down the British in a dispute over Venezuela and its border with British Guiana, and added the 'Roosevelt Corollary' of 1904 to the Monroe Doctrine, insisting that while European forces could not interfere in the domestic affairs of the Americas, the US could do so to prevent or to reverse acts which 'loosened the ties of a civilised society'. This was some distance from any isolationism.

Yet it has to be emphasised that this was once again a matter of controversy internally. By the first decade of the twentieth century, it was the Republican Party that favoured an expansive international approach, while (echoing the row over Empire in Britain in the 1870s and 1880s) the Democrats and the likes of the American Anti-Imperialist League very strongly opposed it. They did not hold the White House or Congress long enough to impose their position on US policy.

Which led to the paradox of Woodrow Wilson as President. As a candidate he had (in accord with the majority of his Democratic Party) opposed militarism, imperialism and interventionism by the United States. He articulated an almost other-worldly liberal internationalism. He stuck with that stance when what would be known as the First World War began, imposing strict neutrality. He ran for re-election (narrowly but successfully) as 'the man who kept us out of the war', implying that the Republicans would be much more likely to enter the fight if restored to the presidency. Within weeks of his second inauguration, he was heading towards participation in the conflict. Less than a year later he was the curator of his 'Fourteen Points' and an advocate of a League of Nations, which the Senate would not accept, and ended his tenure gravely sick, and tragically debilitated by a stroke. If Teddy Roosevelt were yin, then Mr Wilson was yang; neither could impose their Americanism.

The twenty years or so after the end of the Great War are portrayed as a return to isolationism. This is understandable but not a complete picture. It was closer to selective internationalism. The US was active, sometimes hyper-active, diplomatically. It organised (and funded) major humanitarian food aid missions.

It was very involved in the creation of a Permanent Court of International Justice (but did not join it). The Washington Naval Conference spawned a series of naval disarmament schemes during the 1920s. Through the Dawes Plan of 1924 and the Young Plan of 1929, the US sought to reschedule crippling German war reparations. Secretary of State Frank Kellogg co-sponsored the Kellogg–Briand Pact of 1928 renouncing war as an instrument of national policy (for which he was awarded the Nobel Peace Prize). This is hardly isolationism.

Even in the 1930s, remembered for the Neutrality Acts of 1935, 1936, 1937 and then 1939, matters were more subtle than they might seem. Franklin Roosevelt proposed and successfully passed the Lend-Lease Act to supply arms to the Allied powers even before the Japanese attack on Pearl Harbor in December 1941 forced the US into the War.

In all of this time, consistent features remained. America's role in the world turned on what was understood by the term 'Americanism'. This was always disputed. The actions of the United States are not best analysed by a simple divide between isolationism and internationalism.

Profound and persistent security in its borders

All of this is very different from the Chinese notion of a world role rooted in being not so much a country as the oldest continuous civilisation. There are other seminal differences between the US and China as well, not least in the security of borders.

At no moment after 1783 was the United States in danger of drastic territorial reduction. Even the War of 1812 (championed by the Democratic-Republicans led by President Madison and opposed by the Federalists) is not an exception to this. That war was declared by the United States on Britain. A main cause was that the British were convinced that the US had designs on all or part of Canada (well before Mr Trump offered his perspective on that matter). The incursion by British troops into Washington DC in 1814 (and the famed torching of public buildings including the President's Mansion) was not so much an invasion intended to restore the rule of George III, but instead a swift skirmish, and a poor second-best to an assault on Baltimore, which was of much more pivotal military importance. It was the last act in an inconclusive dispute which did not constitute any form of existential menace to the United States and was mostly a tedious distraction for the British from their overwhelming concern, dealing with Napoleonic France. The US has experienced nothing akin to China's angst over the command of its terrain. A few rowdy British soldiers avenging US arson attacks in Canada is not the stuff of the Mongols.

The advance of the United States in the nineteenth century was achieved through the combined effect of acquisition and annexation (sometimes both). It started with the Louisiana Purchase of 1803 from France for the then very sizeable sum of $15 million, territory that stretched far beyond contemporary Louisiana itself and which (once Native Americans were dealt with) opened up the opportunity for the vast extension of yeoman farming, which Mr Jefferson (if not his Federalist rivals) regarded as the whole purpose of the American experiment. To this would be added Florida from Spain in 1819 through the Adams–Onis Treaty. The next push involved the annexation of Texas in 1845. Texas had acquired independence from Mexico nine years earlier but the vexed matter of slavery (which it wished to retain) had led the Democrats (the heirs to Jefferson who favoured inviting Texas in) and the Whigs (the latest variant on the Federalists, who were less enamoured) to fall out over the issue. Buying territory took second place to acquiring it through conquest.

This came through a decisive US victory in the Mexican-American War of 1846–1848. Mexico was obliged not simply to acknowledge the loss of Texas but to concede present-day California, Nevada and Utah as well as segments of what are today Arizona, Colorado, New Mexico and Wyoming. Further sections of Arizona and New Mexico were bought from Mexico in 1854. With a dispute with Britain over the Oregon territory having been resolved satisfactorily, most of what would be the continental United States was in place on the eve of the Civil War (although many territories were not organised into formal states for some time to come). Alaska was bolted on for $7.2 million in 1867; Hawaii incorporated in 1898. If only China could have had it so easy.

The American Century

While China, after literally thousands of years of regional significance and often dominance, had to endure the One Hundred Years of Humiliation, in a quite similar timeframe the United States was instead to enjoy the American Century, which saw the US become a great power.

Dating the American Century, if not as challenging as reaching an agreed accord of what the notion of 'Americanism' actually means, is not as straightforward as it might appear and the debate as to whether the American Century has ended (and if so, when) is absolute quicksand.

The phrase was that of Henry Luce, the publisher of *Life* magazine and *Time* magazine, who in an editorial of

17 February 1941 urged the United States to abandon isolationism outright, enter what was then an essentially European war alongside the United Kingdom and fulfil a role of international leadership which, it was asserted, had long been its obvious destiny.

The beginnings of the American Century could, though, be dated back as far as the late 1860s, with the Civil War resolved and its economy overtaking that of Great Britain itself (but not the entire British Empire) in its size. It could be deemed to have begun about fifty years later, after the American intervention in the First World War had been decisive and its economy had reached a scale where it exceeded the whole British Empire and, by the early 1920s, with New York City having ejected London into second place as the financial capital of the world (where it has been ever since). If so, then the actual centenary of the American Century was reached recently.

The more compelling choice, not least for its neatness, is to take the American victory in the Spanish-American War of 1898 as the initiation of the American Century. It was that event which turned the United States into a power across the Pacific as well as throughout the Atlantic. It rendered the United States, ironically, an anti-imperialist nation in possession of an empire. This would be compounded after the Second World War not only by its new status as an economic, political, military and technological superpower but by a cultural hegemony without historical rival. Hollywood and American television would supplement the US Army, Navy and Air Force.

Has that century come to a conclusion? Probably not, yet. It continued through to at least 2015. In a more qualified form, it has surely lasted to 2025. Can it be sustained all the way to 2049?

Enter the superpower

The United States that evolved after 1941 and even more intensely after 1945 was very distinct from that which had come before it. A conscious decision was taken that instead of avoiding 'entangling alliances' which had been the hallmark of US attitudes even when selective internationalism was largely its mission, the US would instead enable the creation of such alliances, whether they be in the political sphere (the United Nations), the military space (NATO and the US-Japan Treaty) or the economic domain (the IMF and the World Bank). This was a dramatic volte-face for Washington.

It was also, for contingent and somewhat defensive reasons, not a missionary impulse. The USSR was considered an existential threat to the security of the United States like no other nation had been before. Soviet communism was seen as a direct menace to almost any notion of 'Americanism', to the American way of life and to American values. The option of a dignified return to Fortress America and selective internationalism, let alone a fresh embrace of selective isolationism, was not on the table. The menu comprised and would continue to consist of (although it should be said that isolationist dissent on both the Left and the Right would never completely disappear) alternative modes of internationalism as a strategy and between divergent concepts of 'containment' and 'rollback' as related to tactics.

At a point at which China was about to withdraw from the world, the US would fully enter it.

3

THE EAGLE AND THE DRAGON, 1941–2017

A relationship between two countries that at times would be very turbulent started in a positive enough spirit. The first encounter between the United States and China occurred in 1784, before, strictly speaking, the thirteen colonies, then very loosely aligned, became more formally bound by the adoption of a constitution which would come into effect five years later. The visit was well-intentioned, not least because insofar as American cultural and political elites thought of China at all, it was with admiration bordering on reverence. This was also an age of immense strength for the Qing dynasty, when it enjoyed wealth and sophistication that were admired by all of those (admittedly not many) outsiders who reached its shores.

The event itself was the arrival of an American ship, *The Empress of China,* which docked at Guangzhou, then the approved and appropriate place for outsiders who might wish to trade to drop anchor. The exchange was cordial enough and planted the seeds for a trading dialogue, albeit on an extremely small scale. Silk and other luxuries were purchased and returned with the ship to the United States, where the sights reported by the crew entered folklore among upper-class Americans.

This was, unfortunately, something of a high point. There would not be similarly cordial contacts for an extremely long time. Very few Americans set foot in China for the next almost fifty years, until a modest wave of Protestant missionaries started to arrive from 1830. As total outsiders culturally, they were regarded with suspicion.

The Americans were, however, far less of a concern to the Emperor and those around him than the British. As we have seen, the First Opium War had concluded with a humiliating defeat and a settlement in the form of the 1842 Treaty of Nanking, which made massive concessions to Great Britain. It also, alas for China, created a precedent and a blueprint for other foreign powers to push for similarly favourable treatment so as not to be at a disadvantage compared with London.

Although the Americans hardly had might with which to bargain, the Qing were so weak that they seemed to be willing to appease almost anyone in return for a cut of the action. The United States and China thus agreed the Treaty of Wangxia (1844), which offered a deal resembling that which the British had secured, but with enhanced privileges in terms of cabotage (the transport of goods and people between places in the same country) and extraterritoriality, a mechanism by which an external force could obtain an opt-out from laws which applied in a jurisdiction. The US would be in a similar position to obtain yet more after the UK-China Treaty of Tianjin in 1858.

China was still not high on the American priority list as that nation was a long distance away and more concerned with its own divisions (which would explode with the Civil War from 1861 to 1865), and insofar as it had a foreign policy at all, it was to keep the British, French and Spanish (and anyone else who might fancy their chances) out of the Americas. It was only in the 1880s and 1890s, especially after a resounding victory in the Spanish-American War of 1898, that the United States would return to active participation in the affairs of China and on its soil and seas.

There was an exception to this, but it worked the other way round. The direction of human traffic was changing. From the 1840s onwards Chinese labourers (or 'coolies') had started to enter the United States in droves, seeking employment opportunities and undercutting American-born individuals in the process. This was not popular. The response was a series of shamelessly (and shamefully) racist laws that were intended to shut aspiring Chinese workers out on a permanent basis. The Page Act of 1875 instigated the first restrictions on immigration. When it did not stop the flow, it was reinforced by the Chinese Exclusion Act of 1882. When that was deemed not to be watertight enough, the Bayard–Zhang Treaty of 1888 (agreed like most of these items under duress, and in the teeth of the discontent of ordinary Chinese people) sought to stop the supply of those who might want to traverse to the New World by dint of preventing exits. When even that was not thought robust enough, the Geary Act of 1892, reauthorised again a decade later, sent the shutters down so tightly that there was virtually no chance of entry into the US.

While the United States had been absent from the area in the aftermath of its Civil War, a series of foreign powers had hardened their involvement in China and circled each other. The US thus re-entered the scene on the basis of a note authored by Secretary of State John Hay which demanded an 'open door' policy be accepted. The open door concerned was not for China itself but to ensure that the United States could continue to pursue its commercial interests in that country and not be shut out as China was carved up in the same way as the colonialists were doing in Africa. The US was now a credible enough presence in East Asia to insist that its rights were respected.

It intended to defend them with some resolve. American missionaries were among the many foreigners who were caught up in the Boxer Rebellion of 1899–1901 and unceremoniously killed. The US was one of the eight overseas nations that sent troops to put down the rebellion and move the Qing dynasty even deeper into their pockets with de facto surety over China's government. This would only be interrupted by the fall of the Qing, the formation of the Republic (which was feeble from the outset) and the First World War, sending the foreigners back to their own continents. As noted in chapter 1, having supported the victorious side, China thought that it should and would have territories that it had ceded to Germany restored to it, but Japan would have them. This was especially painful as China had already been forced to surrender territory to Tokyo.

Japan would dominate life in China for the next twenty-five years. The United States largely retreated from the region. Not much attention was shown to a China that was rife with internal strife as the Nationalists and Communists competed for authority, and was then invaded from the East. The only US President to offer any succour was Franklin D. Roosevelt, who provided the Nationalists with some financial and military support in their struggle with Japan (the Communists solicited his assistance as well, to no avail), but the scale of his backing was far too small to do much more than very slightly aid the Nationalists in a steep uphill struggle against their invaders.

Roosevelt and Truman from Pearl Harbor to the Korean War

Even before the Japanese struck at Pearl Harbor on 7 December 1941, FDR had been increasing his involvement on behalf of Chiang Kai-Shek and the Nationalists. Through an air campaign known as the 'Flying Tigers', the US had started to edge closer to being an actual combatant in China in order to tie down the Japanese there. Once there was a formal declaration of war, the US considered China to be the land front in its contest with the Japanese, and the flow of arms and money increased very substantially, while on the diplomatic side, the President and his men urged the Nationalists and Communists to suspend their feud and concentrate on the more immediate task (if a difficult one) of dislodging the Japanese Army. At a minimum, if China could hold them down that would buy time for the US to reassemble its forces and prepare, if it were possible, for direct conflict on the ground, not just aerial bombing.

This suited both sides in the civil conflict, arguably the Communists more than their rivals. It saw Mao Zedong (urged on by Joseph Stalin) co-operate fully in this alliance of convenience. The rapprochement with the United States was such that Mao would welcome the main US Army Observation Group to his headquarters at Yan'an in 1944 and suggest that the US might wish to open a consulate there. This did not transpire, and the Americans remained more closely aligned with the Nationalist Kuomintang but could see the argument for the Communists perhaps being brought in as minority partners in a national unity administration once the Japanese had been expelled. Neither Chiang nor Mao was likely to sign up to such a scheme, but that was for later.

The sacrifices that the Chinese people endured between 1941 and 1945 were huge and not unappreciated in the White House. As thinking about the postwar order started in earnest, it was FDR himself who asserted that China should be one of the five victorious powers who would be awarded permanent membership of the forthcoming United Nations Security Council. For a country that did not yet have full command of its own sovereignty and would not until the Japanese surrendered after the atomic bombs were dropped on it in August 1945, this was a heady promotion in the realm of international affairs. When Japan did capitulate, it was obliged to hand Taiwan over to China which, as it turned out, would be of unanticipated significance.

This stance continued after Roosevelt had died in April 1945, with the Truman administration assuming that the Nationalists would automatically acquire command not just in Beijing but throughout the country. The Communists, perhaps nudged along by Stalin who did not seem to be committed to them with any notable resolve, were expected to bring their military resistance to an end and to look for their own lesser but honourable place in a China which, despite all of its past difficulties in dealing with the United States, was now a close and trusted ally. The thought that Mao and his somewhat ragged band might fight and prevail in a renewed civil war was not one that the supposed experts in this field within the State Department took remotely seriously.

It would not be long before they had to revise that opinion. As early as 1947 the Americans began to sense that Chiang was skating on thin ice. By the time of the 1948 election campaign Truman knew privately that the Communists might triumph but there was nothing to be gained from him admitting that on the stump, while Republicans were so (erroneously) confident of victory that they did not ask many questions of him on that matter. Once he had unexpectedly won, Truman cast around for some salvation in China, but other than ordering a full-on invasion in support of Chiang (which did not seem practical), there was little that he could do. The one approach left was to avoid fingers being pointed at the administration if the question of 'Who lost China?' were to be raised in future.

In a rare example of a pre-emptive strike in advance of a defeat that has not yet happened, this is precisely what the White House and the State Department decided to do: absolve themselves of blame before the hour of reckoning. By the summer of 1949 it was openly speculated that Mao was about to run Chiang out of town. In an extremely unconventional move, the administration decided to publish what it called a 'White Paper' under the title 'United States relations with China, with special reference to the period 1944–1949'. It was a stunning document. The main body of the text was 412 pages long, with supporting material in an appendix that involved 642 additional pages. This monumental missive could have been five words – 'it was not our fault'. Secretary of State Dean Acheson lambasted Chiang Kai-Shek for incompetence that had drained support from him. There were harsh words for Mao's insincerity and opportunism too, along with a Letter of Transmittal with Mr Acheson's signature lamenting that it was an especially regrettable state of affairs after the long-standing 'friendship' the US had shown China. That drew hollow laughter from Mao.

It was scarcely the final word on 'Who lost China?' That cry was heard most forcefully from a young Congressman, soon to be Senator, called Richard M. Nixon. It almost certainly created an atmosphere in which McCarthyism could acquire a constituency. Truman was on the back foot.

It would be worse still when conflict erupted in Korea. The North invaded the South but after an initial advance were forced back over the demarcation line, with the prospect that US-led troops might make their way across the entire peninsula, oust Kim Il Sung and the Communists in the North and reunite Korea under American patronage. This was not an outcome that Mao felt he could allow to happen. It would afford the United States a base to attack him at any moment. China thus entered the war with the anaemic alibi that it was not sending in the People's Liberation Army but something else, the People's Volunteer Army, to support North Korea. This changed the facts on the ground significantly. The US and its allies were knocked backwards and had to retreat into the South before fighting their way across the 38th parallel. What was in effect a stalemate then set in, but not before the US dropped 635,000 tons of bombs on North Korea, and obliterated its cities. Truman (wisely) did not seek re-election in 1952. Dwight D. Eisenhower inherited the Korean War.

Eisenhower

He accepted the reality of the situation quickly. The war ended without a treaty as such in 1953. The division of the two Koreas along the 38th parallel was now set in stone. It has stayed there.

This did not render Eisenhower any more open to a reconciliation with Mao or China (not that he was desperate for one either). The focus turned back to Taiwan, which retained the endorsement of the United States that it was the legitimate government of the whole country and hence must continue to hold its permanent seat on the UN Security Council. Mao wanted to do all that he could to undermine the regime across the waters. The United States was resolved to defend it and continued with the hope that Mao himself might be usurped, and a better China re-emerge.

Matters nearly came to blows twice in the 1950s. Eisenhower had lifted the US naval blockade in 1953 which allowed Chiang to send thousands of troops to the strategically significant Quemoy and Matsu islands in the Taiwan Strait in August 1954. Red China reacted to this by shelling the islands on a regular basis. It only desisted after being warned of a nuclear attack. Eisenhower then put his cards on the table by agreeing a mutual defence treaty with Taiwan. If it is possible to draw a line in the sand in water, the President had done so. There would be a near repeat of 1954 in 1958 when again China stopped shelling once told nuclear consequences would follow. Eisenhower doubled down. In his final year in office, he visited Taiwan to an ecstatic welcome.

Kennedy and Johnson

There would be no similar clash between John F. Kennedy and Mao. China was too absorbed by the disastrous effects of the Great Leap Forward and the aftershocks of the Sino-Soviet split of 1960. Mr Kennedy would not have considered this an opportunity to make overtures to Mao anyway. His private and public remarks indicated a deep distrust of China, indeed the fear that it was more radical and reckless than the USSR, and he was doing his best (although it would prove to be futile) to frustrate its self-evident ambitions to acquire a nuclear weapons capacity. He also gave his backing to India when it had a short but sharp border war with China in 1962.

For his successor, Lyndon Johnson, everything to do with China was seen in the context of the Vietnam War. China had not sent in volunteers as active soldiers as it had in Korea, but it was actively offering assistance to North Vietnam by deploying anti-aircraft and engineering experts to repair the damage done by American bombs, thus freeing up resources for the Vietcong. The Cultural Revolution had, in any case, erased the chance of a back channel for negotiation. It was not assumed that much would change when the arch-hawk Richard Nixon replaced him. He had started his ascent by bashing those who had let China slip. He too had the Vietnam War to contend with but said he had a 'secret plan' up his sleeve. It could not involve China, surely?

Nixon goes to China

There was nothing that Nixon could do to salvage the Saigon government, but he could start to recast US foreign policy for when Vietnam stopped being a ball-and-chain for Washington. He seems to have come into office at least toying with the idea of opening up communications, but a notable clash between China and the USSR along their border in 1969 may have spurred him on. He had a soulmate in Henry Kissinger, his National Security Advisor, who had marginalised the Secretary of State as the principal source of counsel on foreign policy within the administration. Kissinger was keen to exploit the improbable popularity of an American table tennis team visiting China in 1971 ('ping pong diplomacy' as it was dubbed) and after claiming illness while in Pakistan went in the utmost secrecy to Beijing to lay the groundwork for Nixon to visit China.

When it was announced in the summer of 1971 that such a trip was scheduled for February 1972 it is hard to say who were the most horrified, the Chinese Left or the American Right. There was dissent inside the CCP, with Mao's heir apparent (Lin Biao) killed in an aircraft crash over Mongolia as he was apparently escaping to defect to the Soviet Union. The former Republican presidential candidate Senator Barry Goldwater led the opposition among the conservatives. They were smarting from Taiwan's ejection from the United Nations and its Security Council.

The Nixon tour was a media spectacular. It would be an overstatement to suggest that the United States and China were to become allies, but they were now in a place which allowed them both to calculate that 'my enemy's enemy is my friend'. Mao was very frail, which limited what could be done with the opening that emerged. Kissinger tried to keep it warm while first Nixon, through disgrace and resignation over Watergate, and then Mao, in dotage and death, departed from the stage. The accidental American President Gerald Ford visited China. A route to recognising Red China existed.

Carter

It would fall to the man who narrowly ousted Ford from the White House to take it over the line. After Mao's death China initially turned inwards. Only when it was clear that Deng Xiaoping, long seen as an able pragmatist and deep sceptic about the motives of the Kremlin in the West, had embedded himself as the Paramount Leader could matters be moved forward again. He came to the United States in 1979 for what was in terms of public relations almost as effective an appearance as that of Nixon at the Great Wall about seven years earlier. He badly wanted to do business with the US. It would jump-start plans to bring his virtually dead economy to life.

His celebrity status in the US made the final push considerably easier. In December 1978, the President announced that Red China would be recognised, and full diplomatic ties embraced. The Taiwan lobby could not block this, but Congress did pass, and Carter agreed to sign, the Taiwan Relations Act of 1979 which meant that the island was not placed in the cold entirely. It also meant the United States' acceptance of the idea of 'One China' was not wholly consistent.

Despite this irritation, after the USSR invaded Afghanistan at the end of 1979, the US and China drew closer still, with Deng making listening stations in Xinjiang available for American usage.

After Carter came a pattern which almost all subsequent presidencies would fall into. When running for President, whether Republican or Democrat but with different scripts, the aspiring candidate would normally be critical of some aspect of the incumbent's engagement with China, but once they were in the hot seat themselves would rapidly revert to the established policy understanding, even if events occasionally threw the relationship into a tailspin. The show was mostly kept on the road, but it could also be too much of a high-wire act for comfort.

Reagan

This formula first manifested itself when Ronald Reagan took over from Mr Carter. When seeking votes in the Republican nomination contest, Mr Reagan was content to let the Taiwan lobby think that he supported them. An extra inducement to do so was that the man who emerged as his main challenger, George H.W. Bush, had once been the de facto US Ambassador to China under Gerald Ford, so was considered by the Taiwan lobby to be suspect in his sentiments.

Mr Reagan kept his act up for longer than was expedient. As President-Elect he made a speech that attacked the People's Republic of China and seemed to be open to reviving the link with Taiwan. Alarm bells rang and an inelegant insistence that his words had been 'misinterpreted' (they had not) was offered to soothe concerns that he was about to reverse Mr Carter's decision.

In the Oval Office, Mr Reagan had an amiable relationship with Deng Xiaoping, although the sheer intensity of the President's anti-Communism, which did not always distinguish between the Russian and Chinese brands, could cause heartburn. He was, however, more than happy to cheer on American corporations that wanted to seek contracts in a rapidly opening China.

This process was assisted by the State Department declaring in 1983 that it considered China to be a 'friendly developing nation'. The President went to China in 1984 and the Chinese Premier reciprocated. Reagan's second term was largely agreeable, although arms sales to Taiwan would always be a hornet's nest and his overtures to Mikhail Gorbachev confused China. The Reagan era was, irrespective of curiosities, essentially a benign one for Deng and for China.

Bush (I)

The relationship between George H.W. Bush and the Chinese leadership should have been a love-in. Mr Bush had lived in

China for a year heading the liaison office (the prototype for what would become the Embassy from 1979 onwards). As a candidate he had no need to distance himself from what the incumbent President had done, as he had been the Vice President. He took the earliest possible chance to land in China in February 1989 in a detour while attending the funeral of Emperor Hirohito of Japan. He received an old friends' reception.

His chance to take the accord to another level was terminated by the Tiananmen Square massacre a matter of months later. Domestic outrage left him with very few options. All official contacts were suspended (although it transpired that he had sent Brent Scowcroft, his trusted National Security Advisor, on a 'fact-finding' mission to Beijing only weeks after the shootings). US–China military collaboration was curtailed. Arms sales ended (they have never resumed). Economic sanctions were imposed. Only towards the end of his term did a dialogue restart.

When it did, it was in the context of a completely changed world. The Berlin Wall had fallen. The Iron Curtain was down. The USSR itself was curtains. While the sudden closure of the Cold War was a cause of celebration in the United States and Europe, although Mr Bush himself kept a diplomatic composure and declined to wrap himself in garlands, it was a matter of anguished soul-searching in Beijing. Deng had been compelled to retreat on reform after Tiananmen. His hardliners pointed to *glasnost* and *perestroika* as the self-inflicted errors which had allowed the Soviet Union to be disposed of without a shot being fired. Deng rejected this and still wanted to return to (economic) reform. Mr Bush, before his defeat in 1992, was keen to back him up again. This would lead to him being attacked from both sides for seeking to engage with the Chinese.

Clinton

Bill Clinton in 1992 did what could be framed as a reverse Reagan from 1980. In his case, it was human rights rather than the treatment of Taiwan that was the catalyst for his criticism. He slammed Mr Bush for 'mollycoddling' China and swore that he would be rather tougher.

At first, he was more distant from Beijing. In May 1993 he signed Executive Order 12850 which linked the continued renewal of China's Most Favoured Nation trading status with its progress on human rights, as defined by the United States. He did not get much in return bar the release of Wei Jingsheng, a political prisoner since 1979. He did agree to another round of armament sales to Taiwan, and Congress further infuriated Beijing, and probably the Chinese public at large, by a high-profile if ultimately impotent resolution opposing China's hosting of the 2000 Olympics. In a slightly slapstick incident, the two countries fell out once more when the US Navy seized the *Yinhe*, a Chinese container ship, alleging that it was transporting illegal material to Iran, but then declined to apologise or, at first, even release the vessel when nothing improper was found on it.

From 1994, with notable exceptions such as when China sought to intimidate Taiwan in advance of its first presidential elections in 1996 and when in 1999 the United States managed to bomb the Chinese Embassy in Belgrade killing five people, the President had largely reverted to the Bush position. He received Jiang Zemin in the US and made his own well-publicised visit to China. It was, more or less and with many an elephant trap in place, close to business as usual. In his final year in office, Mr Clinton signed the US–China Relations Act of 2000, allowing Beijing into the World Trade Organization.

Bush (II)

Despite being his father's son (or because of it), George W. Bush followed the Reagan/Clinton playbook. He was hawkish about China in the nomination competition and had an early mishap of his own when in April 2001 a US EP-3 surveillance aircraft smashed into a Chinese jet fighter over the South China Sea and had to undertake an emergency landing at Hainan Island (part of China). An uncomfortable standoff ensued until Secretary of State Colin Powell uttered the words 'very sorry' to allow the pilot to be released and a line drawn under the incident. All was not forgotten or forgiven when Mr Bush approved arms sales to Taiwan, including submarines.

After 11 September 2001, the Bush outlook was altered entirely. He badly wanted China to be part of his 'War on Terror' and the Chinese had their own reasons to accommodate him. By early 2002, Mr Bush was in Beijing where he spoke of securing a 'constructive' and 'co-operative' relationship. It was all smiles from there on in, including a visit to the Beijing Olympics. Among the areas of intense discussion and tacit accord were North Korea and nuclear weapons.

Obama

American politics towards China had become a broken record. Now it was Barack Obama's turn to be the surly outsider, assailing the outgoing Bush administration less on human rights this time, but rather its trade policy towards China, with the charge that it had turned a blind eye to mass outsourcing, with a harsh effect on US manufacturing. John McCain, his ill-fated

Republican opponent, was a foreign policy expert and said nothing that he might have to reverse later.

Mr Obama began his own repositioning slightly faster than Mr Clinton had done sixteen years earlier. He was in China by November 2009 with a plan to strengthen institutional ties. He lost some of that political capital by agreeing to meet with the Dalai Lama three months later but did so with enough discretion that the Chinese authorities could contain their anger. He signed off on a new 'pivot to Asia' which acknowledged the rising importance of that part of the world but left his Chinese counterparts concerned that America would be interfering further in their sphere.

His own re-election coincided with the anointing of Xi Jinping as the supreme leader in China. An opening for an upgrade in the intensity of the dialogue between the two men was there. They held an atypically lengthy series of meetings in Sunnylands, Rancho Mirage, California. It was billed as the most meaningful such meeting to have been scheduled for four decades. The tone of the talks was considered constructive. The main areas of discord were (as always) arms sales to Taiwan, and what the US saw as China's involvement in the misuse of cybersecurity. Mr Obama wanted to avoid confrontation. During his time as President, a record tally of bilateral agreements would be inked between Washington and Beijing, with climate top of the agenda.

There would be disagreements later. The US was alarmed by China's construction of artificial islands in the South China Sea, designed to add to its claims about where its territorial waters lie and with the utility to become pop-up military bases if required. Such tensions were for the most part contained, although the political temperature was rising. As he prepared to retire after the 2016 election, there seemed to be a Clinton–Bush–Obama consensus.

To almost universal surprise, Donald Trump would become the President after the votes were counted. Entirely predictably as a candidate he had blasted both the incumbent and Hillary Clinton over China, but with trade now a Republican complaint to be levelled at a Democratic President. Mrs Clinton, as a former Secretary of State, and, like Mr McCain, well aware of how the world really worked, sought to sound a touch more sceptical on China than Mr Obama, but said nothing that would need to be unsaid immediately afterwards. Mr Trump meanwhile, in shades of Mr Reagan in 1980, alienated China further by accepting a telephone call as President-Elect from Tsai Ing-wen, the President of Taiwan. But on the basis of American politics over the previous forty years this smacked of form. It was bluster. Normal service would be resumed shortly, wouldn't it?

4

THEORIES, THESES AND TRAPS

An idea whose time has come is irresistible.

Victor Hugo

The economic and political evolution of the United States and China, both separately and in connection with each other, has been a matter of intense intellectual debate as well as public and political discourse. There are times when these realms might appear to be totally detached from one another and others when the link between academia and actions is more explicit.

Not many advocates of either Xi Jinping or Donald Trump would claim that their primary quality is that of being an intel lectual (even if Mr Trump has allegedly been the author of about twenty books and Xi Jinping Thought, his personal take on Marxism-Leninism with Chinese characteristics, has been enshrined in Communist Party doctrine). Neither leader has any apparent impulse to crave the attention and approval of academics in ivory towers (even if there is now a rather substantial cottage industry of explicitly pro-Trump think-tanks within the United States and despite the fact that Xi Jinping retains the services of Wang Huning as his principal ideologist within the Standing Committee of the Politburo). Neither man appears to draw inspiration from a particular philosopher whose works constitute any sort of roadmap. Both leaders regard themselves as extremely practical men, and virtuously so.

This is not to say that ideas do not matter in the context of the US–China relationship or in how international politics is seen more broadly. This chapter seeks to examine the influence of three American figures. One of them used to have a disproportionate steer on official evaluations of foreign policy. The other dealt with a sensitive subject but would be looked at again anew. The third offered by far the most startling critique and has had an impact not only in the United States but also inside China.

The changing of the American mind

There has been a seismic shift in American thinking about China over the past decade. It has occurred within both of the main political parties. For that reason, there was rather more policy continuity over China when Mr Trump was displaced by President Biden than might have been anticipated. Indeed, in many ways the shift has been more substantial in Democratic thinking than among their Republican counterparts, where if nothing else residual anti-Communism meant that a section of the GOP never regarded the economic rise of China as appealing.

The original, broadly bipartisan (with the exception on the Republican Right) analysis of the revitalisation of China as an economic actor was essentially positive. China was not viewed as a systemic rival or threat to the United States in anything like the manner that the USSR had been. There was something almost flattering about a notionally Marxist-Leninist administration in Beijing embracing many of the features of American-style capitalism in order to raise the living standards of the population. The implicit message was that in the battle of ideas between a free-market economy and a planned economy of the traditional Soviet form, both the red flag and the white flag were being waved simultaneously. While in the political sphere, the optimism of Francis Fukuyama's *The End of History and the Last Man* (1992) may have been misplaced, as authoritarians triumphed over old and new democracies across the globe, in economics the struggle was over.

Market triumphalism of itself was not, though, the main moral or political argument in favour of a 'strategic engagement' between the United States and China, which, with comparatively minor amendments, was very largely the hallmark of the approach of every US President from Jimmy Carter to Barack Obama (and would have been followed if there had been a President Dukakis, a President Dole, a President Gore, a President Kerry, a President McCain or indeed a President Romney). The argument that was made constantly and consistently was that, over time, the economic advance of China would, with a rapidly expanding middle class whose support was essential to maintain, lead to incremental but significant political liberalisation within China, which in turn would be to the benefit of peace and prosperity in the world. This was not a process that could be steered from outside or be rushed (memories of Tiananmen Square in 1989 were by themselves robust enough to caution against a sudden democratic surge that would sweep all before it), yet slowly but surely something akin to civil society would become entrenched in China and act as a counterbalance against a crude authoritarianism. Those inclined to look for these trends in the 2000–2010 decade insisted this was occurring.

The assumption that it would has its roots in scholarly interpretation. A number of figures were associated with the assertion of a causal relationship between economic development and the advance of democratic values including key individual human rights, but one academic was perhaps more influential in the enthusiastic advocacy of this notion than the rest of the field.

That individual was Seymour Martin Lipset. He was the son of Russian immigrants and brought up in the hothouse of a mixed immigrant section of New York City. Like many such thinkers at the time he was attracted to neither the Democrats nor the Republicans but to the debate as to exactly which brand of radical socialism was the more virtuous. He was active in the Young People's Socialist League and initially a Trotskyist and resolutely hostile to Stalinism. In later life, following a well-worn path, he would renounce his past association with what he had come to see as a misguided and naive political fringe and instead become a Democrat, and then within their ranks a committed anti-Communist, internationalist and (although he did not care for the label) neo-conservative, which extended his appeal to those aligned with the Republicans.

He was both a political scientist and a sociologist and moved freely between those disciplines. He was the only person ever to serve as both the President of the American Political Science Association (1979–1980) and the American Sociological Association (1992–1993). His stellar academic career included a berth as a Professor at Stanford University and then Harvard University, the latter post bringing his ideas to the attention of, notably, Democrats, be they students or visitors to the university. He was a regular at the Kennedy School of Government.

His contribution to intellectual life ranged widely. He is best known in some quarters for *The First New Nation* (1963), which contended that the United States was the first country to have successfully escaped from colonial rule and that this had shaped its political culture ever since. In that sphere, he was regarded as a founding father in the intellectual (rather than chauvinist, nationalist or emotional) case for American exceptionalism. This had a practical political edge to it. Numerous persons who worked within or alongside the US government were intrigued by what American exceptionalism actually meant and the extent to which it would lead one to either an assertively internationalist or an introspectively isolationist outlook on foreign policy.

In what would come to be the context of the United States and China, Lipset's contribution would be quite different and almost accidental (at the time when he first formulated what would come to be known as the Lipset hypothesis, or the Lipset thesis, the United States and China were so distant and disconnected from one another that the suggestion that his work would have some application to how the two countries might view each other would be entirely implausible).

Lipset was intrigued by the link between economic development and the fostering of democracy. He first sketched out his reasoning in the less than thrillingly entitled *Some Social Requisites of Democracy: Economic Development and Political Legitimacy* (1959). His contention obtained a much larger audience courtesy of *Political Man: The Social Bases of Politics* (1960), through its second chapter on economic development and democracy. At its most basic, he marshalled an argument and evidence that 'the more well-to-do a nation, the greater the chances that it will sustain democracy'. The tome went through several editions, was released in twenty languages and sold 400,000 copies (making it the academic equivalent of a *Harry Potter* book). It was a thesis that he would articulate with considerable rigour and retain many adherents for in the remaining forty-five years of his life.

It made him the leading light of modernisation theory, the notion that modernity was the natural ally, indeed the potential essential prerequisite, for the creation and continuity of democracy. It was an argument that always had its critics, and that served as a catalyst for an at times arcane dispute as to whether democracy occurred endogenously or exogenously, but to a substantial extent Lipset found himself consistently in the limelight.

There was an intuitive logic to what he was postulating. There were not many wealthy nations that were not democracies. There were relatively few poor nations (India was probably the best counterexample but even it could be explained) that were stable democracies. The theoretical and the practical appeared to be at one with each other (not always true in academic thinking). A succession of US administrations, whether they explicitly acknowledged Lipset as the figure behind their activities or not, determined that it was in the national interest of the United States to assist those willing to embrace the economic ethos to succeed in raising living standards. Paradoxically, despite having renounced his own initial political alignment, Lipset was suggesting a causal and inevitable association between economics and politics that could be described as a strain of market Marxism. That might not have bothered him at all.

As late as 2017, although confidence in it was weakening, US policy towards China remained that as China became more integrated into the international economic order, there would be a trickle-down effect in terms of individual liberties and the capacity for political expression. Events, as will be apparent throughout this volume, triggered a sharp reassessment. Even if the Lipset hypothesis held true in many countries across several continents, there appeared to be no firm data to suggest that China was inching towards a more open society. With that changing of the American mind, strategic engagement would not last long as a maxim. It would be displaced by strategic competition at best, or even strategic conflict at the extreme end of the spectrum. If so, then other US-based intellectuals would be more relevant to those conducting politics.

The Rise and Fall of the Great Powers

Science includes the pursuit of a Grand Unified Theory (or theory of everything) within particle physics which would produce a model that merges the electromagnetic, weak and strong forces into a single force at high energy. Much of the work of Professor Stephen Hawking was devoted to reconciling the intellectual evidence in this field, popularised in his *A Brief History of Time*. The frustration is that while many believe that a theory of everything must exist, this unified force has never actually been observed. This will not prevent a continued search.

The study of history has its own versions of the quest for a theory of everything. From ancient times, the nature of power – political, economic, military, technological and cultural – who will hold it, who will retain it, who will eventually lose it, has been of exceptional interest. To reach a conclusion that would have widespread, ideally absolute, application has been a seductive goal. It requires an approach to human history on a massive scale, a truly sweeping argument. In truth, no such thesis is ever destined to satisfy everybody. It is, nonetheless, an attempt at history that both captivates the popular imagination and can influence those who have to devise policies.

A rare example of a book which aspires to make this sort of case, and which caught fire, is *The Rise and Fall of the Great Powers* written by Paul M. Kennedy and published in 1987 (about a year before *A Brief History of Time* reached bookstores; this was a purple patch for visionary academics). It too was translated into numerous languages and sold extremely well. Because of some of its conclusions, though, it has rarely been openly embraced by Americans.

Professor Kennedy himself (born 1945) is actually British by birth although he has lived in the United States for many decades. He became established there after his appointment in 1983 as the J. Richardson Dilworth Professor of British History at Yale University in Connecticut. He later traversed faculties to become the Director of International Security Studies at that institution.

His thesis, to allow it its full title, *The Rise and Fall of the Great Powers: Economic Change and Military Conflict from 1500 to 2000*, was ambitious. It sought to explain why nations rise to become the predominant actor in the international arena for a certain length of time and what then leads them either gradually or rapidly to lose that status, often never to regain it. At its core, his case is that the strength of a great power can only ever be measured in comparative terms relative to other contemporary powers, rather than by any other metric. Seeking to measure up Imperial Spain with the France of Louis XIV with Great Britain after the Industrial Revolution is not an exercise that will extract much of merit. The nature of their supremacies differs. What should intrigue us is why Spain rose and fell, then France and after that Great Britain.

For Kennedy there is a common thread here which runs through the five centuries that he studied. It is the challenge of reconciling available resources, economic durability and military commitments. It is in the end a misalignment or overstretch that leads a great power to take on too much, all but bankrupting itself in what will prove a futile attempt to retain its status. It cannot avoid being displaced by a rival, which will be the pre-eminent power until it too repeats the same mistake that its predecessor made and is eventually sidelined itself by a new successor.

What made the Kennedy thesis somewhat explosive is that while his historical analysis ceased in 1980, he went on to make a series of predictions about what would happen up until 2000. These included his insistence that both the United States and the Soviet Union were heading towards decline, their mutual military overstretching in the end a burden to both of them. He saw Japan continuing to rise, while the jury was out on what was then still termed the European Economic Community (it would not become the European Union until later). Although China was in the early stages of emerging from the chaos of the Mao era, Kennedy had considerable time for Deng Xiaoping's blueprint for his country, notably his proposed Four Modernisations, for agriculture, industry, science and the military, not least because the Professor considered that Deng had put his priorities in precisely the ideal order. China should not seek to invest a major sum in its military until after it had completed the overhaul of the economic fundamentals. So, as early as 1987, the argument was being made that provided China stuck with the Deng format and implemented it rigorously then it was, in the words of the tome, 'only a matter of time' before China not only became important but gained a great power standing.

The thesis that the United States was on the path to decline as a great power rested on the facts that the United States had since the 1960s seen a relative and sharp decline in its share of world production and trade, had declining exports of agricultural produce and manufactured goods and had moved from being the world's largest creditor to the world's largest debtor in a short stretch of time. Furthermore, its federal budget deficit and hence national debt were increasing. The best that American leaders could plausibly do was to engage in a managed, slow decline.

There were many in American academia (and elsewhere) who bought much of this argument. But in Reagan-era America it did not have many cheerleaders in the White House or in Congress. That the USSR was also earmarked for decline was not much compensation. That Japan might still be on the rise struck a raw nerve but suited the spirit of the times as some suggested that it might soon be considered a superpower. That China was expected to surpass all concerned was regarded as an almost outlandish act of intellectual crystal ball gazing. The Professor did not receive red carpet treatment at the White House. Democratic rivals of the administration, particularly those with presidential ambitions, did not rush to endorse his thinking either. It is fair to state that *The Rise and Fall of the Great Powers* was treated far more respectfully in Europe (which had experienced decline) and East Asia (which anticipated its own rise) than it was in the country where the Professor had conducted his research and taught his students.

In fairness to critics of the Kennedy concept, dramatic events over the few years immediately after the publication of his book appeared to undermine the prophecies he had offered. The USSR did not simply decline, it collapsed entirely and had disappeared by the end of 1991, so swiftly that no one saw it coming. The United States was therefore left as the sole superpower and while a recession in 1991–1992 punctured its self-confidence (and cost George H.W. Bush the Oval Office), it recovered its composure and its dominance swiftly. It would enter a benign era that would later be termed and popularised as the 'Great Moderation'.

The rest of the tea leaf reading in the book did not initially appear that inspired either. Japan, far from being on the brink of becoming a superpower, was about to enter a lengthy economic and political malaise that it has barely recovered from more than three-and-a-half decades later. The jury is eternally out on what has become of the European Union, but if forced to record a verdict it would not be a very flattering one. The confidence expressed in the judgement of Deng Xiaoping looked distinctly dubious when he ordered the military to disperse what was by then a relatively small number of dissenting students in Tiananmen Square (probably around 20,000 were left in June 1989, having reached about a million a month or so earlier). Beijing looked set to withdraw once again from the world rather than limber up to take it over.

Much has changed since the 1990–2015 era. What was dubbed the 'Great Moderation' has run its course to be replaced by what I have described elsewhere (in *Trump II: Why He Won. What It Means for the World*) as the 'Great Fragmentation'. What had been an age of undisputed American command over the international order, an international economy in which central banks largely ruled the roost through monetary policy and with globalisation set on a relentless march forward, is no more, but no alternative order appears ready to replace it. The case the Professor made about China today looks rather more astute than it did in 1989.

In that context there is an argument for a further edition and ideally an update of *The Rise and Fall of the Great Powers* to take us all the way to 2050. Much of the argument made by Mr Trump about the need to 'Make America Great Again' has to be based on the rationale that the United States has been great, is no longer great, and has to be restored to greatness. On two of the three metrics that Kennedy identified as indicating that the US was in decline – its falling share of world production and trade and its reduced exports of agricultural and manufacturing goods – both Trump I and emphatically Trump II implicitly recognises the features highlighted and is resolved to act in response to them (there is much less concern about the US continuing to be the largest debtor in the world or the deficit). There will be many in Beijing who agree that it is 'only a matter of time' before it is a real great power.

None of this is to conclude that *The Rise and Fall of the Great Powers* is unambiguously right and should be awarded canonical standing. There is plenty within it that is open to contest. But in the context of the United States and China between 2026 and 2049 it clearly deserves to have a hearing. It offers one vision of how power might or might not change hands between them.

The Thucydides Trap

A drastically different assessment of how the United States and China might interact over the next quarter of this century is the previously discussed 'Thucydides Trap', set out by the final academic under our consideration, Graham Allison. It has been the catalyst for immense deliberation and much disagreement.

Allison has spent his entire career at Harvard University, most prominently as the Douglas Dillon Professor of Government at the John F. Kennedy School of Government. He first made his mark more than fifty years ago with the publication of *Essence of Decision: Explaining the Cuban Missile*

Crisis (1971). In what was a major departure from prior thinking as to how American foreign policy was constructed and delivered, which assumed that the rational actor model explained almost all conduct irrespective of the character or party stripe of the US administration concerned, Allison disagreed and put forward two competing notions instead: an organisational process model and a bureaucratic politics model to explain how the United States and the Soviet Union came close to a nuclear conflict over the missiles installed in Cuba. It was, by academic standards, a revolutionary departure in thinking that won him a wide audience.

The Professor has published widely ever since on the nature of international politics, most recently as the Director of the Belfer Center for Science and International Affairs from 1995 to 2017.

Allison, atypically for an academic, employed an article in the *Financial Times* of 21 August 2012 to warn that the US and China were in danger of falling into the Thucydides Trap as they tested each other out in naval manoeuvres in the South China Sea area. This invoked an observation by Thucydides (c.460–400 BCE) in *History of the Peloponnesian War*, a war which he considered as causing unprecedented suffering to Greece. This war came about, he asserted (although it is not in the original text in these terms), because of 'the rise of Athens and the fear that this inspired in Sparta'. The conflict was less one of choice than a calculation by a dominant power that it needed to strike against a rival on the up while it still had the opportunity, even if the costs of such a move were considerable, the odds of success extremely difficult to calibrate and with the risk that the clash might in fact accelerate Athens' rise, rather than quell it. This was the 'trap' that Allison could see repeating itself between the United States and China.

There had been friction between the United States and China but not much more than that; nevertheless, the argument made a massive splash, even if it did not immediately win a huge number of converts. Allison was making his case at a time when Xi Jinping was still waiting impatiently to assume the leadership of China, while Donald Trump was no more than a businessman and television personality. The notion of a 'trap' appeared an exaggeration. What evidence existed of the inevitability of an actual war in the mid-twenty-first century?

Allison would double down on his argument. It was revisited and reinforced in a 2017 book, *Destined for War: Can America and China Escape Thucydides's Trap?* The Professor did not mince his words, stating emphatically that China and the United States were heading for war. Only deft diplomatic action could avert such a calamity.

This bold, disturbing statement was based on a study that Allison had led at Harvard which examined sixteen examples of an emerging power confronting a ruling power. In twelve of the sixteen case studies, war had followed. The exceptions looked like outliers. These included the contest between Portugal and Spain in the late fifteenth century, the transition of leadership between the United Kingdom and the United States in the 1920s, the dissolution of the USSR which had terminated any prospect of a nuclear or other confrontation with the United States, and (utterly bizarrely) the rise of Germany and the eclipse of the UK and France during the 1990s which showed no sign of resulting in an outright military contest between those nations. In all other instances, such as France versus the Habsburgs in the sixteenth century, France versus Britain in the seventeenth and eighteenth centuries, or the US versus Japan in the twentieth century, the Thucydides Trap held true. There was a compulsion towards conflict.

This analysis was exceptionally controversial. Numerous scholars dived into the examples that had been cited and disputed the findings of the Harvard team or produced counterexamples of their own which had been resolved without rancour. Allison's definitions of 'ruling powers' and 'rising powers' were subjected to demanding scrutiny. The Professor was accused of being an alarmist and having a weaker grasp of military history than he had of modern foreign policy.

The assertion had an effect regardless of what other academics might have thought of it and continues to do so. When Donald Trump hosted Xi Jinping in Washington in April 2017, full-page newspaper advertisements warned the two men of the risks associated with the Thucydides Trap, urging them to see what was coming and work to avoid disharmony. It did not help matters that while American officials and commentators were disinclined to see the US as the contemporary equivalent of Sparta some 2,500 years beforehand, Chinese nationalists (including some in positions of importance) seemed quite content for China to be cast as Athens, at the same time as they insisted that war was neither inevitable, nor did it hold any attraction.

Whether by accident or design, the deployment of the Thucydides Trap into the US–China discourse has altered the overall dialogue. While it is not mentioned much in the corridors of power in Washington DC, it has been discussed endlessly within the Zhongnanhai, the vast Party headquarters which sits next to the old Forbidden City in Beijing. It has been publicly noted by a Chinese Foreign Minister and Defence Minister and cited directly by Xi Jinping in a public forum.

When it is raised it is usually coupled with an appeal to the United States to accept the risk of a Thucydides Trap and avoid the actions that would repeat it. This is less a plea for pacifism or a rejection of the notion that China is indeed a rising power (and the United States a ruling power) than, by implication, a hint that the best course of action would be for Washington to accept its fate and allow for a peaceful rearrangement of roles, as the British did with the US in the 1920s (although that exchange was not entirely serene). As I have previously noted in *A Conservative Revolution?: The Thatcher-Reagan Decade in Perspective* on the history of the UK–US special relationship: 'during the interwar period the US navy devised its war plan Red for execution in the event of a clash with the Royal Navy and Austen Chamberlain, the then Foreign Secretary, informed the Committee on Imperial Defence that while war with Germany, Italy or Japan was inconceivable, war with the United States was not'. It was economic weakness rather than sportsmanship or a sense of fair play that led London to concede authority to Washington (which in turn was not convinced until 1941 that it truly wanted the torch to be passed to it).

As interesting and influential as the writings of Seymour Martin Lipset (who is no longer alive to defend his now unfashionable ideas), Paul M. Kennedy and Graham Allison undoubtedly are, they will not be the people who will determine the course of the US and China as separate players, or in combination with each other. That there is a serious discussion as to whether an armed engagement is either close to inevitable (Allison), an option that cannot be disregarded (Kennedy), or unlikely because economics will in the end be decisive (Lipset), is an indication of how high the stakes are in the years ahead and why the possibilities of war and peace have to be afforded urgent analysis. The decisive actors will be senior politicians. At the outset, this means Xi Jinping for China and, once again, Donald Trump for the United States. If their health holds, the former will probably be there beyond 2027 and the latter until early 2029.

This begs a series of seemingly simple but in practice rather more complicated questions. Who are Xi Jinping and Donald Trump? What accounts for their amazing political ascent? What is it that is distinctive about them as the leaders of China and the United States of America?

5

CHINA IN THE AGE OF XI JINPING

What has been described at the outset as a 'Great Rethink' about China relates to one person.

The vital questions that this chapter will seek to answer are: What explains the actions of Xi Jinping as leader? What is truly distinctive about his rule?

Who is Xi Jinping?

Xi Jinping is the son of Xi Zhongxun. His father had a solid Party pedigree (if not of the very highest rank) and a distinguished military record. By the 1960s, he had a major role in the Party propaganda department but was a relative moderate in the exercise of his authority. He would allow books to be published that others would have banned. He was known to be an admirer of Deng Xiaoping.

So, he was one of the first to suffer under the Cultural Revolution unleashed by Mao Zedong in 1966 in the aftermath of the disaster that was the Great Leap Forward (in reality a Giant Jump Backward that cost around forty million lives to famine). Xi Zhongxun was stripped of office, denounced as a central figure in the so-called 'north-west anti-Party clique' and sent to the countryside to perform menial tasks and experience 're-education'. Almost all allies of Deng were treated in this manner.

At this time, the son was always destined to endure a similar torment to the father. That was the case for Xi Jinping. He became a 'sent-down youth', was compelled to settle in rural Shaanxi province, was obliged to undertake a variety of unappealing occupations and at one stage lived in a cave. He kept attempting to rejoin the Communist Party and its various offshoots, but he was rebuffed. As long as his father was on the (lengthy) list of disapproved persons, then Xi's own chances of being able to return to Beijing, never mind anything close to the life that he had lived before, were minimal. That meant, realistically, waiting for Mao to die and hoping that the Cultural Revolution expired with him. This took place in September 1976.

Enter Deng Xiaoping

Mao's chosen successor, Hua Guofeng, was not a master strategist but had the sense to appreciate that Madame Mao and her closest acolytes were potential trouble for him. He moved very swiftly to have the 'Gang of Four' arrested, imprisoned and then put on what proved to be an almost hypnotic televised show-trial. That was essentially his only achievement as the supreme leader. Within two years he had been comprehensively outwitted by a revived Deng Xiaoping.

Deng was a figure of real stature. He had a past to be proud of. He had become a member of the Party in 1924. He was hence part of a small set of elders later to be known as the 'Eight

Immortals' for their long association with the Party and its coming to power. He would be purged no less than three times and his son paralysed at the hands of a Red Guard mob during the Cultural Revolution. Once Deng finally reached the top, it would allow for a comeback for those like Xi Zhongxun.

Deng fired on all cylinders. He started by reversing the collectivisation of agriculture, permitting peasants who could exceed their quota to sell any surplus to the state or via a market. He then liberalised the environment for academics and intellectuals. He promoted the 'one-child' policy (which had some very awkward side effects later, but dealt with an immediate demographic crisis), he reached out to the United States, and he was very open to foreign investment. He turbocharged the economy through the establishment of Special Economic Zones. One of his allies most closely associated with this was Xi Zhongxun. This would prove to be very helpful to his son later. Deng managed to do all of this while holding very few formal titles. He ran the Central Leadership Advisory Group and was Chairman of the Central Military Commission. He was manifestly in charge, but he championed collective leadership and distributed other roles to a set of supporters, including Hu Yaobang, and later on Zhao Ziyang, both considered to be progressives. Xi Zhongxun was not at that level, but he was on the next rung down. Deng had managed to strip back the Maoist state, while taking care not to be too overtly hostile to the founding father.

Tiananmen Square 1989

The great black spot, however, was the Tiananmen Square massacre of 4 June 1989. It had been triggered by the death of Hu Yaobang, a popular and reforming leader in the early Deng era. Its aftermath was enormous. Zhao Ziyang, who had openly aligned with the student protestors, had to be forced out as General Secretary. The identity of his replacement would speak volumes about whether the Party would continue down Deng's path or go back to that of Mao. Deng managed to move Jiang Zemin, the Shanghai Party supremo, who was independent of, but sympathetic to, him, into this key position, yet the whole system wobbled. Deng Liqun, a full-on leftist, was waiting in the wings if the Party decided to purge his namesake yet again.

Deng put China into permafrost for three years. Once he was confident of his position, he carefully started to resume his reforms but with the emphasis on economics and not political liberalisation. He also intervened to ensure that while Jiang Zemin would serve out the remainder of what would have been his predecessor's full term and would be allowed to be re-elected twice after that, there would be no further extension. It was China's version of the 22nd Amendment to the US Constitution passed in 1951 after Franklin Roosevelt's tenure. Additional checks and balances were also introduced.

The events of 1989, though, still left deep scars. One of those within the Party who had been against them was Xi Zhongxun, who had been even closer to Hu Yaobang than he was to Deng. He was not exactly purged but 'retired' in 1993 (in effect eased out of his official positions) and removed from Beijing, but would live in comfortable conditions for almost a decade until his death in 2002.

The rise of Xi Jinping (part I)

Father and son split over what had been witnessed in Tiananmen Square. There is no evidence that the younger Xi was ever tempted to take a principled stand against Deng because of it. He wanted to pursue a political career through the Party and was therefore content to take the Party line on it. He was determined to get ahead and within twenty-five years he would be in a position to assume power.

His ascent was not smooth nor was it inevitable, despite boasting considerable advantages. He had a reasonably famous family name, even if he was not directly descended from one of the 'Eight Immortals'. He worked very hard and acquired a reputation for competence. He had something of the common touch to him. He appears to have been sincerely opposed to corruption and not corrupt personally.

His other vital ally was his wife, Peng Liyuan. For much of the time after their marriage (his second) in 1987, she was more famous than he was. She was the daughter of a leading figure in the military who had been purged during the Cultural Revolution, condemned as one of the 'five black elements' and sent, with his children, to the 'cowshed' in the countryside. He and she were treated even more harshly than the older and younger Xi had been. When he was later rehabilitated (under Deng), she was able to come back to the capital and demonstrate a startling talent, that of singing. She became a television sensation with an impressive ability to hit notes of great height. There is no US or European figure to compare her with perfectly, but Barbra Streisand is a respectable fit.

Xi started to rise but it was not all straightforward. His political career began in Hebei province, the region that largely surrounds Beijing. He stood for the Central Committee in 1997 but came 151st in the contest for 150 openly elected slots. This embarrassment was resolved by an extra place being invented for him. He moved on to take the helm of Fujian province, on the south coast of China. From there he would take over in

Zhejiang province, its eastern neighbour. After that was a short stint in charge of Shanghai. He was closing in on becoming chosen as the Party leader heir apparent to be selected in 2007.

Waiting in the wings

The role of heir apparent has proved a very vulnerable one in Chinese Communist Party politics. It was no guarantee of ultimate victory. There were a number of developments that could have put paid to his aspirations and opened the door for a new candidate to emerge as an alternative. The 2008 Beijing Olympics, for which Xi was in charge of preparations, could have undermined him if they were considered a failure, but they were deemed a triumph.

As matters evolved, three different crises occurred which could have proved politically fatal for Xi. They are partly interconnected and explain the kind of leader he became.

The first was a set of riots by the Uyghurs of Xinjiang province in July 2009. This area, in the very far north-west of China, has never been easy for Beijing to administer. The uprising was eventually suppressed, but there is no doubt that the Party was shaken. It boosted spending on the security services by a considerable margin and publicly blamed foreigners for having whipped up discontent.

The second issue to emerge was ideological in character. In 2012, the Development Research Center of the State Council and the World Bank released a report entitled 'China 2030: Building a Modern, Harmonious and Creative Society'. The Left of the Party hated it. Some 1,644 economists wrote an open letter condemning its heresies. Xi had to distance himself from the study.

The final threat was more personal. It was the meteoric rise of Bo Xilai as a candidate for leader. Xi had a number of reasons to fear him. Bo's father, Bo Yibo, was one of the 'Eight Immortals', indeed the last of them to die in early 2007 at the age of ninety-eight. Bo was hence a proper 'princeling', which Xi was not. He was a highly charismatic figure with a flair for positive self-publicity. He was making a splash in charge of Chongqing from 2007 onwards. He was also becoming a darling of the Maoists.

Bo's fall, however, was as fast as his rise. It was in 2012, the year in which, in November, the Party would settle on a new General Secretary and Chairman of the Central Military Commission. Lurid suggestions of corruption started to be made of Bo (they probably had some legitimacy). In a very strange twist to the plot, Bo was linked via his wife to the murder of Neil Heywood, a British businessman with whom she was known to have had dealings. Bo was arrested, imprisoned, put on trial, expelled from the Party and sentenced to life imprisonment. He is still in jail somewhere.

Xi was understandably cautious as the pivotal Party Congress drew closer. He had to ensure that absolutely everything would run smoothly and to his script. It went exactly the way that he wanted it. He had two of the three key positions. He would add that of State President in March 2013, a post that was supposed to come with a term limit of two five-year periods in office. He was very clearly and very firmly established as the Paramount Leader.

The rise of Xi Jinping (part II)

It did not take long for what would be the primary hallmarks of Xi's rule to become apparent. The first was an incredible centralisation of authority in his own hands. Whereas Deng had eschewed titles, Xi collected them like some people seek out postage stamps. He is known as the 'Chairman of Everything', running four of the eight most significant formal committees and inventing others such as the Leading Group on Overall Reform, which cut across conventional Party and state structures. On 17 March 2018, the National People's Congress re-elected him as State President, but without the prohibition against him seeking any further extension of his tenure. On Christmas Day 2019, a moment when we now know that Covid-19 must have been sweeping across and beyond Wuhan, the Politburo officially named him as the 'People's Leader'. Only Mao had that accolade before.

The crucial element here is that previous Chinese leaders from Deng onwards were subject to checks and balances, a strong element of collective leadership and term limits on the office of President. This was one-party rule, not one-person rule, which had been tested to destruction under Mao. It meant that everyone in the system knew that there would be a transition after ten years. That would ensure that a strong leader became weaker as his time ran out.

The rise of Xi Jinping (part III)

This is no longer the case. The National People's Congress re-elected him to a third term in October 2022. It also approved a radical shake-up of the Standing Committee of the Politburo with Li Qiang, the former head of the Shanghai region, coming in as the second-ranked member, and hence serving in effect as Premier, an extremely unusual promotion as he had not served on the Standing Committee before. His elevation did not, however, make him an heir apparent. Indeed, although a talented administrator and engaging figure on most accounts, his vigorous implementation of a 'Zero Covid' stance in China's largest city had rendered him distinctly unpopular. Those of a more conspiratorial bent therefore deduced that Xi had deliberately alighted upon a number two who would serve him with some distinction but would find it very hard indeed to be seen as a successor. If so, then, ironically, within weeks of his appointment being announced, Li Qiang had been at the heart of a huge policy switch in which the original official stance on enforcing Zero Covid was to all intents and purposes jettisoned, largely, it can be presumed, in response to public opposition.

Nonetheless, the rise of Xi Jinping appeared even more robust. He had held the three most important posts in Chinese politics (General Secretary of the Communist Party, Chairman of the Central Military Commission and State President) for a decade and was now destined (if his health held) to do so for a further five years with no obvious obstacle to an additional extension that would take him beyond 2027 and 2028, when his mandates would need to be renewed once more. Although the suggestion of 'President for Life' appeared a long stretch (unless he died in office), it was clearly a major departure from the limitations on personal rule that Deng had intended to be built into the system on a permanent basis to prevent the Party becoming the property of one person. This alone would make Xi Jinping an atypically important leader in recent Chinese history.

It is, though, not the only sense in which he would depart from the 'Deng Model', even if the notion of him as the reincarnation of Chairman Mao would be a caricature. The first Chinese President to be born after 1949 aspired to shape the

China to be seen come 2049. Whereas his immediate predecessors might have been incrementalists on almost everything except a remorseless focus on economic growth and the living standards of the public, he was more radical.

The distinctive features of Xi Jinping as the leader of China

It is now reasonably clear that Xi Jinping had a firm view of what he thought was right and wrong with the now ageing Deng Model that he had inherited. More significantly, he knew what he wanted to do to correct and improve it.

The 'Xi Effect' has been so fundamental in the short term in many regards that seeking to organise his tenure's features into distinct categories inevitably requires an element of simplification. The essential point is that they do represent a coherent and consistent outlook on public life and while there are some surprising, even potentially contradictory, aspects to them, they most surely amount to a belief system; indeed they are knocking on the door of a full-blown ideological stance.

Once Xi had assumed full control, he saw three real challenges.

The first was that the Party itself did not have the hold on Chinese society that it once had. This was due in large part to the fact that the ruthless pragmatism which had been the hallmark of Deng begged the question of what the CCP stood for. Ideology (of which Deng was rarely an enthusiast, having been on the receiving end of far too much of it personally) had been thoroughly marginalised.

The second was that while China had become much more prosperous in the period since Deng had assumed overall charge, it was also, by 2013, vastly more unequal in the distribution of economic spoils. There were (particularly for a supposedly Communist nation) astonishing economic disparities at the personal level, at the regional level and to a degree at the generational level. Some in the ruling elite either had not noticed this or were not concerned about it, or had concluded that it was a temporary phase to be endured which would correct itself as China matured as an economy. The new leader saw this as an extremely dangerous development and one that had to be addressed.

The third, which was to some extent related to or the by-product of the second, was that the 'dash for growth' by the fastest possible route, with success being measured by the date at which China might overtake the United States as the largest economy in the world (thus 'mission accomplished'), was not as satisfying a strategy as might have been thought by those who ploughed Deng's furrow. China should want to be more than a mass manufacturer of high-volume, low-value products aimed predominantly at Western consumers, but with a reliance on others for the economic basics (energy supplies) and the technologies (semiconductor chips) essential for thousands of factories that now existed to build and deliver their wares. The China of the future should at a minimum become far more self-sufficient and, ideally, should become an innovator, a genuine leader in high technology. It should also want to shape the global polity rather than be shaped by a system.

This was the background to what can be considered the five main features of Xi Jinping's leadership thus far.

Reasserting the Party by renewing ideology

The new leader wanted from the outset to revive the Party by rediscovering its Marxist-Leninist soul. The earliest indication of this came in what, when it was leaked a matter of months into his tenure, became known as 'Document Number 9' or, more specifically, 'A Communique on the Current State of the Ideological Sphere'. In essence, the new supremo was not much impressed. The CCP was not only failing to make the case for Marxism-Leninism, it appeared to be almost embarrassed at the notion of doing so. As a result, Western (for which one could read American) notions of constitutional democracy and a separation of powers, universal values such as human rights, civil society as a force in itself, a free press, the logic of political reform following economic reform and, at worst, neo-liberalism and the supremacy of market principles were becoming part of the informal discourse, especially for younger and more educated citizens.

The Xi era has seen an enormous effort to revive not merely the Party as an institution but the core principles of Marxist-Leninist teaching (albeit with 'Chinese characteristics') within its approach. This in turn has led to the formal incorporation of Xi Jinping Thought not only into the central tenets of the Party itself but the national constitution. Although often portrayed as a Mao-style personality cult, it is actually better considered a cult of the Party rather than of its leader. Mao had a love-hate relationship with the Party (as the Cultural Revolution demonstrated starkly). Xi Jinping is far more interested in reviving the relationship between the Party and its purpose and the population. The reassertion of ideology has left rather less room for anything else within public discourse. It would not be accurate to claim that dissent has been extinguished, but debate is to occur within the Party and not about the Party. Democracy is to be deemed one of, perhaps the most lethal of, the 'Five Poisons' that China faces (the others being Uyghur activists, Tibetan separatism, those who advocate

Taiwanese independence and, although it seems to be under control, the Falun Gong movement).

The credibility of this enterprise has also come hand in hand with another hallmark of the Xi age. There have been numerous anti-corruption campaigns during the CCP's time in charge of China. Most have been half-hearted and short-lived, but since 2013 they have been deep and continuous.

Connecting the Party to a wider narrative of Chinese history

The CCP has often appeared uncertain about its relationship with Chinese history. China and the Chinese have a deeply developed sense of that history and the continuous character of their civilisation (even if others would not read the evidence in exactly the manner that they do). Yet its long history mostly involves Emperors and philosophers and religions or spiritualities that do not sit comfortably with a Marxist-Leninist mindset. Some within the Party have long been tempted (in a less chilling manner than Pol Pot in Cambodia in the 1970s) to treat 1949 as a form of 'Year Zero' with most of what went before to be dismissed as inconsequential or without attraction. Others have just ignored the past and concentrated on the immediate present and the future.

Despite his determination to reinvigorate ideology, Xi appears to be much more relaxed about the previous history of the country and about presenting Marxism-Leninism as part of a longer continuum. He has been, for example, the first Party leader to embrace Confucius, openly marking his birthday. He has been ready to talk about the importance of Buddhism in national development. In an article for *Qiushi*, the key Party journal, published in October 2023, he referred to China as the Earth's 'only great, uninterrupted, civilisation that continues to this day in a state form'. He is thus both a radical in insisting upon the continued, indeed enhanced, importance of Marxist-Leninist ideology and also, in a sense, a conservative traditionalist and nationalist. It is an intriguing combination.

Revising the balance within market socialism

There is not much doubt that Xi is a relative sceptic about the 'market' element of 'market socialism'. He is not a capitalist in Communist clothing. He started his time in power with a determination to curb what he perceived as the already rampant excesses of the Deng Model as it had evolved in the fifteen years or so since its creator had expired. His desire to do so would be reinforced by a spectacular stock market crash in 2015, which wiped out the savings of millions of citizens and which the Party appeared to be powerless to prevent. He disliked the rise of capitalist celebrities who might be seen as alternative sources of wisdom and leadership to the Party itself. This became plain when Jack Ma, the poster child for the Chinese super-wealthy and founder of Alibaba, was brought to heel after criticising Chinese regulators for impeding his activities. He would disappear from view (making a modest return in 2025) and the campaign thoroughly spooked private entrepreneurs across China and, even more spectacularly, external investors in the country. The leader did not mind this. He did not echo Deng's notion that to be rich was to be glorious. His mantra is 'common prosperity'.

The new ethos was demonstrated in the fourteenth Five-Year Plan adopted for the 2021–2025 period. It came after the centenary of the foundation of the CCP, with the Party congratulating itself that it had turned China into a 'moderately prosperous society' but now needing to turn its attention to 2049 (with 2035 identified as a mid-point) when it would be a fully developed economy and nation.

It drew a clear line between the 'real economy' and the 'fictitious economy' (the latter located in financial and property speculation). It offered a vision of China's future structured around Xi's own 'New Development Concept' and his identification in 2017 of a new 'principal contradiction' (or primary challenge) for the Party and the nation, namely 'the contradiction between unbalanced and inadequate development and the people's ever-growing need for a better life'. From here on in, the Plan argued, the motor of the economy would be increased domestic consumer demand and not exports of the lowest common denominator. Implementing this in reality would not be easy.

The target growth rates for the economy would be pegged back and what growth consisted of, and not simply the headline figure itself, would be awarded more significance. The Deng Model had produced socially menacing sources of instability and left the Party in a weaker position to guide Chinese society in its favoured direction. In short, less 'market' and more 'socialism'.

From high volume to high technology

The proportions of 'market' and 'socialism' were not the only issue on the Xi Jinping economic agenda. As observed earlier, he was far from convinced that the country would become a global powerhouse by producing millions of cheap clothes and toys for Western consumers or being the first port of call for white goods such as refrigerators and dishwashers. This was not merely a form of distaste at satisfying the materialism of others (China was also selling this sort of output at home) but reflected a concern about what has been christened the 'middle income trap', the prospect that after a spectacular period of expansion, an economy becomes caught in an awkward no-man's-land. It is neither as cheap as it once was (which would allow the likes of Vietnam, Indonesia and the Philippines in time to undercut it), nor is it sufficiently advanced enough to compete with the likes of the United States and Europe in the realm of high-value transformative technology. Xi did not want China to be the new Hong Kong. A larger version of Japan, South Korea or even (but whisper it softly) Taiwan was a much more inspiring notion. Growth in itself might be a dead end.

Again, with the advantage of hindsight, this shift in outlook was hiding in plain sight. As early as 2015, a 'Made in China 2025' plan was framed and launched, outlining the need for self-sufficiency in key sectors and an overall upgrade in the entire structure of the (less market-centric) Chinese economy. The Deng Model had served its purpose to the point of being counterproductive. Change was coming.

A new role for China in the world

The new leader intended to depart from the Deng Model abroad as well. For the better part of thirty-five years, China's foreign policy and its sense of its role in the world had followed on from his maxim that the country should 'hide your strength, bide your time, never take the lead'. On paper, Beijing, not least because it was a permanent member of the United Nations Security Council, could take a pivotal role in international affairs and, in the abstract at least, might push against the rules-based order that largely reflected US leadership. In practice, it did not do this.

From the start of his rule, Xi Jinping had bigger and bolder ambitions for China on the global stage. He would press China's national interests more emphatically in disputes with its neighbours (on border and territorial arguments at sea). He would champion the modernisation of the military (which had not been a central issue for his post-Deng predecessors). He would stake out a new authority in economic development via the Belt and Road Initiative, which was one of his first signature policies when he acquired his office and which has been a mainstay of Chinese foreign policy ever since, vastly increasing its influence in Central Asia, Africa and much of Latin America. China would be an advocate for turning the BRICS (Brazil, Russia, India, China and South Africa) into something more than a zippy acronym and into an alternative to the G7 as an economic actor. He would encourage much more intense Chinese participation in the internal activities of the United Nations, the World Bank and the International Monetary Fund, and the machinery of the World Trade Organization (and, although it became a source of controversy during the Covid-19 pandemic, the World Health Organization). In a myriad of other institutions where China had been virtually invisible, it acquired a new profile. This was not to be a campaign of stealth. China wanted others to know that it had arrived on the scene.

This would mean, unavoidably, an element of tension with the United States. Xi was both critical of and fascinated by this systemic rival (his only child, a daughter, attended Harvard University). He had a cordial relationship with Barack Obama but sought a 'new type of great power relationship', as was set out, albeit subtly, at a summit with the US President in 2013. The Chinese President spoke of a 'community of common destiny', different from a Pax Americana. He was determined that the rise of China should be recognised, respected and registered. He stood for 'national rejuvenation' and hence sought to be a 'global leader'. No more keeping China's head down.

When added together, the reassertion of the Party and its ideology, a willingness to incorporate this into a wider story of Chinese history, a revision of the balance between 'market' and 'socialism', the drive to upgrade Chinese economic output and a far more assertive attitude to foreign affairs are a seismic recasting of China as a country. It certainly made Xi Jinping the most significant leader of his country since the death of Deng in 1997. Whether he can achieve what he wants is another matter.

6

THE UNITED STATES IN THE AGE OF DONALD TRUMP

To an extraordinary degree the story of American politics over the past decade has been that of one man, Donald J. Trump. This was even true when he was out of office and a virtual pariah between 2021 and 2025, such was the probability that he would seek and regain the Republican nomination for 2024, and such were the massive difficulties with President Joe Biden making a successful bid for a second term when he would be eighty-six years old, if he managed to complete it.

If in January 2015 anyone had said that Mr Trump would stand for the Oval Office in 2016, secure the Republican nomination relatively easily, defeat the vastly more experienced politician that was ex-First Lady, ex-Senator, ex-Secretary of State Hillary Clinton with a solid margin in the electoral college but fewer popular votes, serve as President for a term before being defeated, but refuse to accept or acknowledge that loss, then stand once more and breeze his way to the nomination before beating the incumbent Vice President not only in the electoral college but in the popular vote as well, few would have thought such a course of events credible. It could not be likened to a script of *The West Wing*, because it would have been too implausible a storyline ever to be broadcast.

Yet this is exactly where American political and public life may stand until 20 January 2029.

Who is Donald Trump?

There was not much about the first almost seven decades of Mr Trump's life that suggested he was destined to occupy the White House. He was the fourth of five children born to Fred Trump, a New York City real estate figure, and Mary Anne MacLeod Trump, of Scottish heritage. He was the second son, but his older brother, Fred Trump Jr, had little enthusiasm for entering the family business despite his father doing his utmost to conscript him into it. The eldest son wanted instead to become an airline pilot (which he did) but that fell well below the sights that Fred Trump Sr had for him. The two became estranged; Fred Jr lapsed into alcoholism and was dead at the age of forty-two. The second son was unambiguously the one to lead the company.

Which indeed he did, but from early on it was clear that he had quite a different vision for what had been called Trump Management but was soon to be renamed (by the young Donald) The Trump Organization. It would be harsh to describe Fred Trump as a slum landlord, but it would be fair to assert that he specialised in commercial and some residential property that was in the less visually attractive end of the market. His residents were of middling to lower incomes.

The son had a more ambitious agenda. He wanted the big, the bold and the beautiful. His first major project involved the wholesale renovation of the Commodore Hotel, a prime site smack next to Grand Central Terminal. It would reopen as the bright and brash Grand Hyatt Hotel in 1980. In that same year, Mr Trump obtained the right to develop what would be Trump Tower, once again right in the very heart of Manhattan. He then moved on to similarly opulent hotels elsewhere in the United States and beyond, to casinos, to private clubs such as the Mar-a-Lago estate in Florida which he bought for a relative steal in the 1980s and then later revamped, to golf courses and a slew of other ventures that had a more chequered track record of success. In every instance, the entity concerned sported the word TRUMP in capital letters and in gold leaf.

The unsurprising and not unwelcome consequence of this was that he became a public figure and a media celebrity. His lively private life and natural showmanship made him a magnet to the New York City newspapers which were then read in vastly larger numbers than they are today. He broadened his appeal by penning *The Art of the Deal* in 1987, which was a rare example of a book that was theoretically destined for the business shelves being placed in the front window. From 1996 to 2015 he owned all or part of the Miss Universe franchise which included Miss USA and Miss Teen USA. He further developed his television profile by hosting the hugely popular American version of *The Apprentice*, which introduced him to millions of viewers.

While his exact wealth remained something of a mystery (and the accounts of The Trump Organization are strikingly opaque), he had become part of American public life and discourse. This did not, of itself, make him a plausible contender to be the President of the United States.

He did, though, have an interest in politics and public policy. As early as 1987 he had taken out full-page newspaper advertisements to set out his views on the federal budget deficit and on foreign policy. He had dropped hints that he would be willing to be considered as George H.W. Bush's vice-presidential running mate in 1988 (an idea that the candidate himself deemed crazy). Having been a registered Republican from 1987 to 1999, he became disenchanted with them. He aligned himself with the Reform Party of Ross Perot and Patrick J. Buchanan and briefly explored the prospect of becoming their presidential candidate in 2000. When it became evident that either this would not occur or, if selected, he would be a marginal contender, he withdrew from the electoral arena. He would not think about it again for over a decade.

Although his association with the Reform Party now appears distinctly odd, there was in retrospect a logic to it. Mr Perot and Mr Buchanan were deeply sceptical about pure free market economics, the merits of free trade and a missionary American role in international politics. Much of what they stood for then would later be imposed on the Republicans by Mr Trump.

Enter George W. Bush

There was no love lost at any point between the Bush family and Mr Trump. Almost as soon as George W. Bush had been sworn in as President, Mr Trump switched his registration once again, this time to become a Democrat which he was between 2001 and 2009, although with no clear enthusiasm for seeking office under that affiliation. It was, nevertheless, the ultimate trajectory of the Bush administration which created an opening for Mr Trump to launch what was in effect a hostile takeover bid for the Republican Party in the aftermath of the Bush era.

Mr Bush was in most respects an orthodox post-Reagan Republican (more so than his father who had more of an

Eisenhower–Nixon set of instincts). He favoured free markets, free trade and light-touch regulation as far as possible. He was a social conservative who courted the religious Right and hinted that he would use Supreme Court appointments on his watch to engineer the overturning of the contentious *Roe v. Wade* 1973 ruling on abortion. He was initially cautious on foreign policy but after 9/11, he became an advocate of hard power and proactive intervention overseas, with the seemingly successful incursion into Afghanistan and subsequent invasion of Iraq signalling a muscular approach to international relations with the forceful promotion of democracy as its mission. For a time, this credo not only dominated Republican thinking, but was shaping the world order. It was some distance away from the arguments that Mr Trump had made in the 1980s and 1990s.

It would all come crashing down. The last months of the Bush administration were taken up by seeking to minimise the damage of the global financial crisis that emerged in late 2008. The entire US banking system and with it, potentially, the economy as a whole, had been brought to its knees by the collapse of Lehman Brothers. This in turn exposed the extent to which the wider financial system was at risk of a total breakdown due to poorly regulated or unregulated lending. The faith that Mr Bush had placed in free markets, free trade and minimalist regulation looked misplaced. The Republican Party as a whole, which had echoed these tunes, found itself losing its gospel.

Social conservatives were not that much more satisfied after the eight Bush years either. There had been two Supreme Court appointments and while both were seen as solid conservative choices (views about Chief Justice John Roberts in evangelical circles would change over time), the actual balance of the court had not shifted. There seemed to be no more probability of *Roe v. Wade* being discarded in 2008 than there had been when Bill Clinton vacated 1600 Pennsylvania Avenue. On a personal level, the Christian Right liked Mr Bush, but he had not delivered for them. If and when the Republicans were defeated in his aftermath, a reassessment would be needed.

It was in foreign policy, however, that the demise of what had become Republican orthodoxy under Mr Bush was the most dramatic. The intervention in Iraq became a nightmare. The United States was pouring men and money into that country and receiving little in return. The notion that it might provide a beacon for democracy in the Middle East was clearly ridiculous. If there was a victor at all from the overthrow of Saddam Hussein, then it was not the US but Iran, which was able to exert influence through speaking to the Shia majority in Iraq. The situation in Afghanistan was not much more palatable. An enormous outside presence headed by the United States could just about keep the Taliban out, but the country was ungovernable. It was unclear whether the Republican vision for the United States in the world had any currency.

In short, by 2009, the Republicans had a void in economic, social and foreign policy. The initial reaction to this was the Tea Party movement, an attempt to restore the Party to first principles. That initiative lacked a leader (Mr Trump dropped the hint in 2011 that he might be available but did not receive a calling), attracted too many fringe figures, and lacked specific measures. After their landslide victory in the elections to the House of Representatives in 2010, the GOP set about the more immediate task of denying Barack Obama a second term of office. Out of a thin field, Mitt Romney, a candidate more respected than revered, was selected. He sought to paper over the (many) internal cracks and to focus on the economy, but he was defeated. The ideological anguish and uncertainty of the Republicans had by 2013 intensified further still.

The rise of Donald Trump (part I)

In June 2015, Mr Trump descended from his luxurious apartment at Trump Tower to declare his candidacy for the Republican nomination for President. It was not widely expected at this stage that he would win that race. His stance had the air of a publicity stunt. The track record of businessmen turned aspiring Commanders-in-Chief was not stellar. The likes of Steve Forbes, Herman Cain and even, in a way, Mr Romney, had not become President (although Mr Romney had managed to take the nomination at the second time of asking in 2012). It was uncertain whether Mr Trump had any kind of organisation to back up his name recognition. The thought of him pressing the flesh in the early states of Iowa and New Hampshire, where very personal engagement with small numbers of electors is the expected campaigning technique, strained credibility. His multiple marriages would, it was said, deter the Christian Right.

Besides which, ex-Governor of Florida, Jeb Bush, the establishment favourite, was about to run. He seemed much better placed to vanquish Hillary Clinton, the near-certain Democratic nominee, and become the third member of the Bush dynasty to raise his hand to take the oath of office.

Matters did not evolve as the Republican hierarchy had imagined. Mr Bush barely made it out of the starting blocks before withdrawing. There would be a splintered field (as many as seventeen candidates at one point) which assisted Mr Trump no end and made the emergence of a single alternative to him much harder. His message, one that would have been heresy to many Republicans a decade earlier, had a large audience. His innovation of very large rallies rather than voter-by-voter handshaking and schmoozing worked well enough even in Iowa to allow him to claim second place there and keep his momentum going, and did him no harm whatsoever in New Hampshire where he comfortably won that vital Primary. Once he had stormed home again in South Carolina, he was teed up to sweep Super Tuesday. Only John Kasich, the Governor of Ohio, sought to stay in the contest. He had no realistic chance. A stunned Republican Party found itself with Mr Trump as its nominee. A distinctly strange convention had anointed him. It seemed, though, that Mrs Clinton would have the measure of him.

Yet again, conventional wisdom took a beating. Neither of the options were that popular. Both were polarising personalities (albeit for separate reasons). The Democratic contender invariably led in the national opinion polls but not by the margin that one expected. The campaign was error-prone. She seemingly fainted at one point. There was a raucous set of debates. He appeared to have been sunk when a tape emerged of him suggesting denigrating sexual tactics towards women. The experts agreed come election day that while Mrs Clinton would not win by much, she would be the victor. The markets suggested that she had an 83 per cent chance.

It did not happen. The distance in the popular vote was closer than the opinion polls signalled (a mere 2 per cent advantage for Mrs Clinton, not the 4–6 per cent that the printed numbers were indicating). She was also winning her votes in the wrong places, racking up oversized majorities in the likes of California and New York but falling short in Michigan, Pennsylvania and Wisconsin. With Mr Trump also narrowly ahead in the softer states of the South (Georgia, North Carolina, Florida), he was on course for victory. It was hardly by acclamation. The exit polls stated that he had a 36 per cent approval rating but 46 per cent of the vote and 306 electoral votes compared to Clinton's 232.

The outcome seemed to stun Team Trump (insofar as there was such a collective). With the Republicans having held on to a solid majority in the House of Representatives and retaining their control of the Senate, Mr Trump had not only won but was set fair to make the weather. The enormity of all this suddenly became apparent. He was barely prepared. He had no relevant background for the responsibilities that would very shortly come. It would be the Apprentice Presidency.

The rise (and seeming demise) of Donald Trump (part II)

The first term of the Trump administration was in many respects a rather chaotic affair. Those recruited to the White House and throughout the executive were an assemblage of personal contacts, a few figures from the campaign (such as the alt-right Steve Bannon) and a host of others whom the new President scarcely knew, or in other cases did not know at all. The transition team (headed up by Chris Christie, the former Governor of New Jersey) either had not done its work or had been steamrollered by others. The opening days of the Trump I era had an anarchic element to them. The Inauguration Address was more akin to a campaign rally with the most memorable phrase uttered being the words 'American carnage'. An unseemly row broke out between the new Press Secretary and the media as to whether more or fewer ordinary citizens had attended Mr Trump's swearing-in or the first Obama inauguration in 2009. As part of this (entirely unnecessary) war of words, the concept of 'alternative facts' was put into the public domain by Kellyanne Conway, Counsellor to the President, in a *Meet the Press* interview and roundly mocked thereafter. It appeared that a parallel Trump universe was emerging.

This was the pattern of the first two years of the Trump White House. The President was largely an orthodox Republican in domestic matters (his signature Tax Cuts and Jobs Act of 2017, the most substantial legislative accomplishment of his tenure, was mainstream Republicanism). Where he broke from the past was mostly in international economics (although his drive for tariffs would meet internal resistance) and international relations (of which more later). This was all undermined by feuding among his own appointees. His initial Secretary of State (Rex Tillerson) left after little more than a year (fired by tweet), the opening National Security Advisor (Michael Flynn) was ejected inside a month, his first Chief of Staff (Reince Priebus) made it to six months, and the contentious Steve Bannon's time as Chief Strategist was about four weeks longer. The absolute record for minimal political life expectancy was secured by Anthony Scaramucci, who lasted as White House Communications Director for ten days.

Despite this, Mr Trump entered the year 2020 with a reasonable prospect of re-election. The White House had calmed down. He had been through an exceptionally steep learning curve. The economy was still positive. There was no stand-out figure among his Democratic opponents and if there was a favourite at all, it was probably Senator Bernie Sanders, a self-styled socialist. His approval ratings had edged up to 49 per cent, the highest that he had obtained and enough to win.

The arrival of Covid-19 changed everything. After an initial reticence, Mr Trump had to introduce measures that would shutter sections of the economy and induce a temporary recession. The Democrats did not choose Senator Sanders but ex-Vice President Joe Biden, a safer option if even then his age and mental agility might be scrutinised. The pandemic meant that normal campaigning was impossible. The best hope for the incumbent was to roll the dice and fund the swift emergence of a vaccine, which he did (but not in time for Election Day). With a far more limited social safety net for citizens than in Europe, crucial sections of the electorate were hurt.

Although once more the national opinion polls underestimated him, the President lost both in the popular vote (by 4.4 per cent) and in the electoral college where the 2016 numbers were flipped. Mr Trump did not concede. He instead seemed intent on disputing the outcome and was seen by many as inciting a crowd of supporters he addressed in Washington to march on Capitol Hill, storm the building itself and so seek to prevent the ratification of the election result. Mr Trump declined to attend his successor's inauguration and was impeached (for the second time) by the House of Representatives (but not convicted by two-thirds of the Senate). It was an ugly spectacle. He retreated to Florida (not New York). It looked to be all over for him.

The rise of Donald Trump (part III)

Like Mark Twain, reports of Donald Trump's (political) death turned out to be exaggerated. He would lie low for a short while before making it obvious that he would mount a comeback. He did so despite discouraging polling numbers nationally, the manifest disapproval of much of the Republican Party in Congress and elsewhere, and a roster of court appearances on a variety of federal and state criminal and civil charges. He led the nomination race from the start (even though he declined to appear in the debates with the other contenders) and once he had won in Iowa, New Hampshire and South Carolina, the nomination became a coronation. To the horror of the Republican establishment, they would once again be obliged to rally around an interloper.

Although tight (but not as close as had been widely predicted), his return to office was relatively smooth. He survived an assassination attempt on the eve of the Republican convention by literally millimetres. He received a hero's welcome from the delegates and made Senator JD Vance of Ohio his vice-presidential contender. He was then thrown off course when President Biden finally recognised the inevitable and withdrew very late in the day in favour of his Vice President, Kamala Harris, who acquired the nomination unopposed. The ex-President took time to adjust to his new rival but eventually hit his stride. The intense support of his base, the unpopularity of the sitting President and widespread concern about the economy were all in his favour. He prevailed in the popular vote and resurrected the electoral college map of 2016 (with the addition of Nevada). With the Republicans holding the Senate and (by a minuscule edge) the House of Representatives, he would soon prove to be a master of Washington politics this time.

The distinctive features of Donald Trump as President of the United States

Mr Trump is a very different President from not only his Democratic but also his Republican immediate predecessors. Trump II is also likely to be different from Trump I and is better thought of as a second first term in office rather than what a standard second term of office would usually be. The restored Trump White House has already shown itself to be better organised and more ideological in its approach than the original example. When Mr Trump first entered the Oval Office, he did so with little more than a set of slogans. In 2025, he came back in with a strategy.

There are (at least) five distinctive features of Donald Trump as President of the United States which in an unexpected manner have similarities to the 'Xi effect' on the leadership of China.

A new form of Republicanism

The closest equivalent in the United States to the sort of manifesto seen in Britain and Europe is the Party platform endorsed at the national convention every four years. The 2016 document was a lengthy and uneasy combination of mainstream Republican thinking and the campaign themes with which Mr Trump had obtained the nomination (to the hostility of many in the Party). The pandemic meant that no normal convention could be held in 2020, so no new platform was issued; instead, they referred to that of 2016. The platform adopted in July 2024, not a programme as such but a line of travel, was the first chance for Trump Republicanism to appear.

That document is entitled 'America First: A Return to Common Sense' and represents a decisive break from the approach and outlook that would have been associated with every GOP nominee from Ronald Reagan in 1980 to Mitt Romney in 2012. It is much more strident in its tone and apocalyptic about the prospects of the country if the Democrats were to continue to control it. There is a much stronger emphasis on the political power of the presidency as an institution. The virtues of tax cuts are extolled (as one would expect) but there is far less interest in deficit cutting. Social, but more forcefully cultural, conservatism is extolled along with an attack on 'wokeism'. The foreign policy section (as will be outlined) is the most radical departure of the platform.

A REVERSION TO THE REPUBLICANISM OF A DIFFERENT ERA

While Trumpism is new, in that it is a departure from the Republican Party of the previous four decades or so, it is also old in that many of his arguments hark back to an earlier Republican outlook that had been almost forgotten.

There are many examples of this. One is a kind of anti-politician politics, with Mr Trump's status as an 'outsider saviour'; it would have chimed with Republicans for much of their history. Much of what is within 'America First' as a creed, often framed by proponents and opponents alike as nationalism, nativism, populism, protectionism, isolationism and unilateralism, would have been normal political fodder for the Republican Party a century previously. In the 1920s, Republicans selected prominent business figures to their leadership, recruited the very richest men to sit in the Cabinet, railed against inadequate control of the borders and sought to limit the supply of unappealing immigrants (mostly Irish and East European Roman Catholics then), aspired to spread prosperity among the citizenry and were wary of outside engagements (hence their rejection of the League of Nations) but vigilant in enforcing the Monroe Doctrine of US supremacy within the Americas. Mr Trump is hence not a deviation from Republicanism but a reversion to a form of it that had been lost after the New Deal, Second World War and Cold War.

Rebalancing free market economics

Mr Trump is not a Wall Street Republican. He will accept sizeable funding from any financial institution willing to lend it to him (functioning off debt raises no issues with him, whether it be for The Trump Organization or the US Treasury) but he is not of that corporate mindset. He likes to build things and, to that extent, like Xi Jinping, favours the 'real economy' over a 'fictitious economy'. If free market economics damages the American manufacturing sector, then Mr Trump is against it.

There is thus a strong streak of populism in his economic message. A sky-high stock market is a worthwhile outcome not because it enriches those who trade on it but because it boosts the retirement savings of millions of ordinary Americans. A short-term dip in stocks, if that comes as a consequence of other initiatives that he undertakes, will not deter him from his objectives. A little inflation (but not excessively so) can at times be of tactical convenience. Tax cuts are a good in their own right which should be at least partially offset by spending restraint (but not if it involves interfering with the politically sacrosanct such as Medicare). Debt is fine provided that it can eventually be financed (although that is more of a dilemma for creditors than for debtors). It is an approach to domestic economic policy that has the added value of affording flexibility.

From free trade to tariffs

Mr Trump is even more sceptical (actually, far more sceptical) on free trade than free markets. He starts from the premise that a trade deficit in goods (which the United States persistently has) is a bad state of affairs. While others have convinced themselves that the Trump stance on tariffs is all bluster, a negotiating ploy to obtain incrementally better outcomes within the free trade system, a closer examination of the President's record and rhetoric would not lead to that conclusion.

His stance would be better summarised by a single sentence in the 2024 Republican Party platform. It is:

> For decades, our politicians sold our jobs and livelihoods to the highest bidder overseas with unfair trade deals and a blind faith in the siren song of globalisation.

This is a stark view of international economics but one to which Mr Trump has hewed for a long time. He would almost certainly have wished to take more domineering action on tariffs during his first term. However, the absence of strong supporters of that position around him and, at that time, a shortage of intellectual ammunition from sympathetic think-tanks, meant he could not do more than modestly renegotiate the old North American Free Trade Agreement and start a trade war of sorts with China, for which the groundwork had not been adequately laid. With his return, although there has been some unease inside the administration, tariffs are not just serious but central and essential to his wider vision for the revitalisation of US manufacturing. That became clear on tariff 'Liberation Day' (2 April 2025), even if the success or failure of that initiative (curbed somewhat shortly afterwards) will be uncertain for some time yet.

This also puts many Democrats in a bind as they too have bailed out on globalisation (and did so before the Republicans under Trump), which limits their ability to stand in the way of tariffs. If the Trump White House can extract anything from their deployment, then tariffs will be here to stay.

A new role for the United States in the world

The Trump II era is thus likely to be a radical one for the conduct of international economics. It will be no less seminal for international relations. This again is an instance where the instincts of the President in his opening term, which could not be fully transmitted into deeds, will not be diluted or obstructed at the second time of asking. Mr Trump believes that the end of the Cold War should have led, but did not, to a fundamental cost–benefit re-evaluation of US foreign policy. He has no zeal for what he sees as the freeloading of others (notably in Europe) on the American taxpayer for military expenditures. He has little time for what he regards as pointless and endless wars whether they be in Ukraine (which the US has heavily funded) or in the Middle East (he will avoid Afghanistan, Iraq and Syria like the plague), nor does he see why the United States should not pursue its interests unilaterally rather than in muted multilateralism.

As a by-product of this approach, Mr Trump is a comparative moderate in his own camp over China. His concern is the bilateral trade deficit (by far the largest that the US has with any trading partner). How Beijing handles the Uyghurs, Tibetan activists or Falun Gong is of scant concern to him (though harassment of Christians within China does aggrieve his own Party). He does not share the ideological opposition to a larger role for China in international affairs that Marco Rubio, his Secretary of State, articulated frequently when still serving in the Senate.

Put together, Mr Trump's determination to replace recent Republican orthodoxy with 'America First', his reversion to themes of the Republican Party of the 1920s and 1930s (and earlier), his willingness to doubt the absolute sanctity of a free market ethos on economics, his outright opposition to free trade and embrace of tariffs and what is a Trump Doctrine on foreign affairs is a seriously transformational shift in American politics. How much is implemented is to be seen.

There is clearly no shortage of ambition, even if consistency of direction can be hard to discern. Mr Trump's definition of 'America First' is a flexible one. Any doubt on this score was surely settled in the early months of 2026 when he first authorised a raid on Venezuela and captured President Nicolás Maduro, then threatened to seize Greenland from Denmark before, alongside Israel, launching an astonishing attack on Iran and the Islamic Republic. This was by far his largest armed intervention to date and the most controversial. China would not have been alone in asking 'what next?' and 'where next?'.

This unilateral activism demonstrated Mr Trump's capacity to overturn the international order seemingly at will. It also exposed doubts and divisions within his own 'Make America Great Again' movement, the wider Republican Party and the US public over what the role of the United States in the world should be. It is a question with a very long history and still no consensus as to the correct answer. These tensions were downplayed at the cordial Xi-Trump summit in Beijing in May 2026 but they have not disappeared.

7

THE NUMBERS GAME

Demography, it is often stated, 'is destiny'. This is, in fact, far too sweeping a statement. Demographic factors clearly influence a society and an economy. They only become fundamental in relatively extreme circumstances.

There are, nonetheless, some basics about demographics and demographic change that do tell a story. Whether a country's population is rising or falling is one such indicator. The fertility rate is of legitimate interest. The gender balance, if deviant from the international norm, might hold clues to something worth exploring. The age distribution and, in advanced economies, the direction of the so-called dependency ratio, the number of people of working age compared with those who are either too young (normally thought of as zero to fourteen years of age) or too old (usually deemed to be sixty-five years of age and older, very roughly) to expect to be in full-time employment, can be truly revealing. Whether a country is changing in terms of its racial or ethnic composition is also well worth contemplating. When all of these variables appear to be moving in the same approximate direction, then it is reasonable to make some estimates as to what that might mean for an economy and for the ease of managing a society.

People are not then prisoners of demographics. What might appear to be fundamentals can and do change. Added to which, the total number of human beings is not the only consideration. Their lives are shaped by technological innovations and external shocks, such as wars on a massive scale, unforeseen pandemics (as Covid-19 demonstrated) and, potentially, dramatic climate change. These will oblige people and countries to alter their perceptions and their behaviour. That in turn can upend what beforehand might have appeared to be near certainties in their demographics. Too many ultimately false arguments are made due to taking a line on a chart and deciding that it will continue remorselessly in the same direction.

Comparing the United States and China, 2026–2049

Despite all those health warnings, a comparison between the United States and China over the second quarter of this century has to start with demographics before it can move on to anything else. This should not be done in a blinkered fashion. The numbers game partly explains why the United States has the largest economy in the world but, as it is far from the most populous part of this planet, it can hardly be the primary cause. The astonishing rise of China as an economy over the past forty years is not because its already massive population surged to become several times larger (indeed, as will be set out here, a systematic drive at population restraint occurred at exactly the same time as output per person was shooting skywards). There will be more to the next twenty-five years than what the census each decade, and the interim estimates between censuses, seem to tell us. Nevertheless, the allure of extrapolating from data is often all but irresistible.

The very broad outlines of the comparison made here are as follows. These are not two countries that have followed similar trajectories over the last seventy-five years, nor even the last twenty-five years, and they will not be tracking each other over the next twenty-five years, or possibly seventy-five years (as just argued, we should avoid seeking to divine the future much beyond a single generation). The differences in what has been witnessed are more compelling than the (few) similarities.

This is partly because of geography. Asia holds the majority of humanity. It has nine nations with populations that are well over that of, say, the United Kingdom. That is far less true for North America, where the United States has clearly the largest population (even if one counts, as one probably should, Mexico as North America, not Central America, for this exercise). The United States including Alaska is larger than China (without Alaska, the other forty-eight states of the continental US plus Hawaii are actually smaller) but the population overall and its density of population (almost a quarter of that of China – 37 people per square kilometre, compared to 151) are smaller. China's density would be even more intense were it not for Xinjiang province, which is vast but inhabited by only a tiny fraction of all Chinese citizens. Demography should pay all due respect to geography if it is to be viewed in the right context.

The one-child policy

It also needs to take heed of politics and public administration. The biggest single reason by far for the very different demographics that we are expecting to see in the United States and

China between 2026 and 2049 is that one of these countries introduced a one-child policy between 1979 and 2015, while the other did not and it would have been inconceivable for it to have done so.

The importance of the one-child policy and its subsequent ramifications for the fate of China is such that it is well worth examining how and why it came about and why it has both succeeded and failed.

China has long been used to having a very large population relative to the rest of the world (often extremely so). In the year 1500, as an example, it is believed to have had a population not that far from 300 million, at a time when Tudor England probably contained no more than three million. Exactly how large the Chinese population has been in absolute terms and as a proportion of the global tally has waxed and waned according to social and economic stability in the country itself, shocks such as the flooding of its great rivers which in ancient times were its lifeblood, and the effectiveness or not of harvests (famine has been a terrifyingly consistent factor in the history of the country). The idea before the CCP alighted on the theme in the late 1970s that one could attempt to fine-tune the population level would have been ridiculous.

This was true when the People's Republic was declared in 1949. The previous three decades or more had been among the most tumultuous in Chinese history. The country was in such bad shape then that no census could realistically be conducted in anything akin to a professional manner (and this in a nation where, in the second century CE, the rulers of the Han dynasty recorded the oldest surviving census data anywhere in human history, identifying a population of 57.7 million people living in 12.4 million households). Events meant that census-taking was abandoned. Estimates of the numbers in that era are based on far too little information with almost no independent means of verification available. They are at best an exceedingly general indicator, but one that would not stand up to scrutiny. In the same vein, any figures offered for GDP should be taken with a sizeable pinch of salt. These were the Dark Ages for those who want to know precisely what China's statistics were.

If nothing else, the CCP has brought some discipline into this theatre. Since it seized power, there has been a national census of some credibility in its conduct and its conclusions in 1953, 1964, 1982 (the eighteen-year gap reflects the turmoil caused by the Cultural Revolution), 1990, 2000, 2010 and 2020 (it is instructive that only at the end of the twentieth century was China adequately developed and stable for what has been the norm in Europe and North America since the nineteenth century: a census every ten years).

China was to see a population spurt under the People's Republic. The best available estimate (allowing for the rather wayward process set out above) is that it went from around 550 million people in the very early 1950s to 970 million in the very late 1970s and is thought to have topped the one billion mark (the first country ever to do so) a few years later in 1982.

At first, the authorities were not displeased by this situation. A large and expanding population might be held up as a virtue, a sign of success, a resource that might be mobilised for China. That initial sentiment was soon reconsidered and the full challenge of how to feed an ever-increasing number of mouths came to haunt the senior leadership. There were several family planning campaigns organised from the 1950s onwards. Given the rise in population over the next quarter-century, they do not seem to have been effective. This was an overwhelmingly agricultural society, and more hands were needed for physical labour. Access to contraception in rural areas was unavoidably limited and, in any case, there was cultural resistance to it. Sadly, the only population control drive that the CCP managed to carry out that worked during these decades was the Great Leap Forward which delivered (if that is the right term), through an avoidable famine, that which all its family planning initiatives could not.

By the time that Deng had become Paramount Leader in 1978 there was a real sense that the population figures would spiral out of control with catastrophic implications. Almost as a last throw of the dice, the Party latched on to the one-child policy, although strictly speaking it was one child in urban areas and two children in rural locations and some ethnic minorities were allowed an exemption (probably because it would have been virtually impossible to enforce).

There were significant financial incentives to toe the line and hefty sanctions if a family did not co-operate. As early as 1982, 96 per cent of families in cities were having one child only. The rewards were so enticing that even in rural China it made economic sense to agree to settle on a single child despite the rules stating that two children would be accepted. In the context of farming, unfortunately, a son was more important to have than a daughter. The CCP found itself turning a blind eye as late abortions and the sudden deaths of girls after birth became almost the norm in certain communities. What this meant was not thought through.

Hence, as will be set out here, the one-child policy was at the same time a fantastic success and a monumental failure. It was a success in that it realised what was supposed to be its mission: ending an era of uncontrollable population growth and restoring demographic order. It was a failure in that the side-effects of this policy became so dramatic that the policy was not only discarded but triggered a rush to correct for its many deficiencies.

This becomes apparent when a comparison between China and the United States is made.

The population of China is falling, that of the United States is increasing

The population of China peaked in about 2021 at around 1.42 billion after several years of incremental growth and has slipped back since that point. It is now in decline. In 2024, it was 1.41 billion, or 17.2 per cent of the overall planet. It had a negative growth rate in that year of –0.15 per cent. The first official estimate for 2025 suggested that it had slipped by another three million in that year. More stunningly, only 5.63 births per 1,000 people were recorded (the weakest figure ever). In raw numbers, this meant 7.92 million babies born (down 17 per cent on 2024). The (in popular superstition) ill-fated Year of the Snake was (implausibly) blamed for the fall.

Shortly before this, in late 2023, it had been confirmed that India rather than China was now home to the most people in the world (whether this is an accolade to be cherished is contestable). There is no reason to dispute that claim (and sound grounds to accept it), but if so then it is the first time in many centuries (plausibly so far back in human history that we are knocking on the door of the Bronze Age) that what we think of today as China has not been the most populous society in the world. It would have been unimaginable in 1982.

The population is set to fall further. It will be somewhere around 1.398 billion in 2030 when the growth rate will be -0.25 per cent, 1.343 billion in 2040 with a growth rate of

-0.45 per cent and 1.260 billion in 2050 with a growth rate of -0.71 per cent. If one wants to embrace the estimates that stretch further into the future than that (which would be heroic), then projections for China's population in the last quarter of this century fall to somewhere between 650 million and 900 million (or where it was in either about 1955 or 1975, depending on which figures we opt to venerate). Much as there has never been a rise in population on the scale that China has enjoyed or endured in human history before, this will be a decline on a scale that has never been experienced either.

A crash of this sort is of more than passing concern to those who like large populations. Much of China's economic strides relative to the United States have been down to having vastly more people who were shifting from the countryside into the cities (the number of urban Chinese increased from 26 per cent in 1990 to 67 per cent in 2024, a staggering switch) and becoming more productive in terms of measured output as they entered conurbations. This factor has run out of road.

The unspoken truth is that if one looks at the fertility rate, although it was abolished in 2015, China still has a one-child policy, except that is not because of any decision issued by the General Secretary of the Communist Party, but because people, most relevantly women, have made that decision themselves. The fertility rate in China now rests somewhere between 1.1 and 1.2 (the standard accepted number to ensure a stable population is 2.1). The last (debateable) official figure of 1.3 dates back to 2020. It is close to the lowest in the world (South Korea seems to be a little smaller). It has become set in stone.

This is for several reasons. There are too many men and too few women and that remains in the system. The sex ratio – the number of men for every 100 women – among men aged twenty-three to thirty-seven and women aged twenty-two to thirty-six (the ages when more than 80 per cent of each sex who do marry get married; having a child outside of wedlock in China is rare) will hit what is hoped to be a peak of 119 in 2027. In 2012, only fifteen years earlier than this assumed spike, it was just 105, very much smaller. The share of unmarried men in this prime age group had risen from about 13 per cent to around 30 per cent between 2006 and 2022. This is a really seismic increase in a not particularly lengthy time.

Even if a man and a woman of the appropriate age do get married and intend to have a child together, it is unlikely that they will reproduce to the extent that Beijing might want them to. One might imagine that, in a Communist country, there would be free or subsidised provision of the most important services for family life and the rearing of children – schools and healthcare – and that the economics of starting a family would not be that draconian a calculation. If that is the assumption, then it is very much mistaken. The cost of raising a child in China starts at about seven times its per capita GDP, arguably the highest such figure in the world (it is only four times per capita GDP in the United States). For anyone outside the wealthiest bracket of the population, one child is a financial handful. One plausible assertion puts the cost of a child at over $75,000. A second child would be an unbearable strain on family resources. This is compounded by an extremely competitive approach to schooling, frequently involving expensive private tutoring, which further hammers family finances.

China's population is thus on the slide and will keep on sliding. The population of the United States, as a long-established developed nation, also has its demographic challenges but not on anything like this order of magnitude. The population is steadily increasing (it rose by almost 1 per cent between 2023 and 2024) as a large wave of immigration earlier this century is now feeding its way through to the age groups most likely to produce children. The American fertility rate is much closer to 1.7 than 1.1 or 1.2, and among certain segments of the population (young Hispanics) it is close to the replacement rate of 2.1. As long as legal immigration does not become as politically unpopular as illegal immigration is as of now, then the United States has plenty of scope to supplement an underwhelming fertility rate with more citizens from other places.

The sex ratio in China remains suspicious when it should have normalised

A warped gender ratio was a manifest and malign side-effect of the one-child dictum and a major factor in why it had to be tossed aside. In the years immediately before that reversal, it was often 118 males to 100 females, which was perplexing when the country had become far less rural, which should have removed one of the main reasons for preferring sons over daughters. By now, this contorted sex ratio should have worked its way out of the social structure. It has to a degree, but the gender ratio at birth is still misaligned at 110 males to 100 females for which there is no compelling biological explanation. It seems like not only is there still a de facto one-child policy under the radar, but it is one with a bias in favour of boys, almost certainly assisted by the most liberal abortion laws in the world and by all counts the most visited abortion clinics. The sex ratio in the United States was, as of 2024, 104.5 males to 100 females, which is where it should be. For every year that China deviates from that sort of number it will have difficulties twenty-five to thirty-five years later when a new cohort reaches the age when they would marry and decide on having a family. There is no similar challenge of this kind at all facing the United States now, or in the future.

China's population is not only decreasing, it is ageing rapidly

The decline in China's population is, in the short term, essentially incremental, although that will not be the case at about mid-century. What is more sensational is how swiftly it is ageing. This will almost certainly be the largest single social problem that the nation will encounter.

The numbers are utterly mind-boggling.

As of 2023, China's population by age group was as follows. Those aged zero to fourteen years (who are too young to work legally) represent 16.8 per cent of the total. Those aged fifteen to sixty-four (the classic working age segment) constitute 68.9 per cent of the overall figure. Those who are sixty-five and older (usually not in full-time employment) are the remaining 14.3 per cent. Those aged eighty and beyond (probably the most dependent on others for social assistance) are a relatively small 2.5 per cent of Chinese people.

Those numbers are not drastically different from those of the United States in 2024. The zero- to fourteen-year-olds there were 18.2 per cent of the population. Those aged fifteen to sixty-four were 64.9 per cent and those aged sixty-five and older came in at 16.9 per cent. Those who had attained eighty years of age or more were 2.9 per cent. The US thus has more younger people (proportionately) than China and more older people but fewer in the middle and hence a smaller percentage who would constitute the working-age population. That similarity might surprise some people, but it does not suggest that China should be anxious.

This is the calm before the storm. It is what will happen over the short term and medium term (much of which is demographically baked in, as it were) that will constitute a revolution.

By 2030, in China, the zero to fourteen section will have declined to 13.1 per cent. The fifteen to sixty-four section will edge down very slightly to 68.7 per cent and the sixty-five and over will increase markedly to 18.2 per cent. What one might impolitely label the very old (eighty years and counting) will have nudged up to 3.5 per cent. The working-age population will not have altered much, but while in 2023 there were more young people below that cohort than there were older persons above it, by 2030 there will not be.

It is twenty years after this that the dam is set to burst. By 2050, the youngest section will have sunk to 11.4 per cent. Those aged fifteen to sixty-four will have reduced notably to 58.5 per cent. Senior citizens will comprise 30.1 per cent, with the very oldest fraternity (eighty and over) coming in at 10.3 per cent. It is hard to overstate what a massive transformation of society this will be. In 2023 there were almost seven times as many young people (zero to fourteen) as very old people (eighty and over). By 2050, they will make up almost the same proportions of the population. Nothing like this is projected for the United States. There will be some shrinkage in the working-age population, but the young are not about to disappear while the eldest become ever more dominant. The change in the US is subtle.

If these figures seem like an implausible earthquake that cannot possibly transpire in fact, consider this aspect of the evidence. It took China forty-four years from 1978 to 2022 to see the percentage of its population who were aged sixty-five or more increase from 7 per cent to 14 per cent. It took the United States sixty-nine years from 1944 to 2013 to do the same. The ageing of the Chinese public is happening at warp speed. There is little if anything that can be done about the trend (bar the extermination of the elderly, which would hardly arrest the overall fall in the population).

What this in turn means is that the median age of the population will increase substantially. As of today, it is forty (similar to the United States but very slightly higher). By 2030 it will be 42.7. In 2050 it is set to be 50.7. The numbers for the United States will also ease upwards (as they will throughout the developed world, probably more aggressively in Europe than North America, although there will be considerable variation by individual nation) but 'ease' is the correct term here. The change will be much more gradual, and gentle, and can be tempered if the authorities become uneasy about it by turning on the (legal) immigration taps (the demand to become an American is enormous).

This safety valve is not available in China which has extremely low immigration (net migration statistically), shows absolutely no appetite for wanting to attract immigration and even if it did (which is highly improbable) would not be a magnet for immigration (with the exception of those trapped in North Korea who might come over in droves if they were offered that escape hatch). In a typical year, the United States issues 750 times the number of permanent residency permits that China does and has the further incentive of the English language as well.

Not only are there certain to be more older people in China (in percentage terms) but they are living much longer. This is a development for which the country surely deserves applause. It has been wildly successful in this area. Chinese life expectancy has surged from a miserable tally of only thirty-five years when the Chinese Communist Party came to power in 1949 to seventy-seven today and 79.2 years at birth. This is comparable with the United States (where lifestyle habits constrict its life expectancy despite its wealth as a country) and only just below the OECD average (not bad for a country that is developing rather than fully developed). This is a phenomenal outcome.

It will get better still (but with social effects as part of the process). Life expectancy at birth is expected to motor on from 79.2 in 2025 to 80.2 in 2030 to 83.7 in 2050. If anything, this is more likely to be an underestimate than an overestimate. If younger Chinese people follow the Western pattern and (unlike their forebears) eschew cigarette smoking, then it is entirely possible that life expectancy will be even higher than these projections.

This is not, it should be repeated, a negative development. On the contrary, it should be cheered to the rafters. But it means that the China of the second quarter of the twenty-first century will be a society that is quite distinct from the first quarter of the same century, vastly changed from the last quarter of the twentieth century and so removed from the quarter before that (the first quarter-century after Mao had secured control of the country and restored its unity and sovereignty) as to be almost two completely different nations. The China of 2026–2049 will be transformed. The life experience of China's citizens will be transformed.

Is China ready for this? The most fundamental statistics of them all relate to the potential old-age support ratios, in this instance expressed as those aged twenty to sixty-four compared with those who are sixty-five and over (the numbers of those who are fifteen to nineteen, who are really part of the full-time working-age population in China, are small and getting smaller due to low numbers and the desire to remain in full-time education for longer). Put brutally, this is a figure that tells one how many people of working age are supporting how many who have exited the workforce. Back in 1965 this was 12.5. In 2025 it had fallen to 4.3. In 2030 it will be about 3.4. In 2050 it should be around 1.8. There will be nothing remotely like this seen in the United States in either 2030 or 2050.

The first stirrings of the realisation that society will have to be reordered have been registered. It will not be a comfortable process. The numbers relating to the working-age population are even worse than they look because, for reasons of historical legacy from when life expectancy was far lower than it is now, the retirement age in China has been what looks almost comically low.

The relevant age for female blue-collar workers is currently fifty. For female white-collar workers it is fifty-five (the temptation to swap into a blue-collar role after the age of forty-five must be attractive). For men, the standard retirement age is sixty. This makes a mockery of the notion that the working-age population is in practice anything like what the statisticians are portraying it as being in theory.

This cannot continue. After years of prevarication and with the minimum amount of publicity as it would not be a popular move, the Chinese authorities announced in 2024 (whispered would be more accurate) that the retirement age of female blue-collar workers would be increased between 2025 and 2040 to fifty-five, that for white-collar female workers from fifty-five to fifty-eight, and for all men from sixty to sixty-three. Assuming that this is implemented (and there must be some doubt about that), these would still be extraordinarily charitable retirement ages. The typical Chinese citizen would become economically inactive (even if nominally still part of a working-age population) earlier than their counterparts in the United States or all of Europe (even including France).

This is part of a wider strategy that might be politely described as scattergun. In 2025, it was announced that there would be a state subsidy of 3,600 yuan (or £400) annually for each child under three years of age. Kindergartens, day care centres, even some dating agencies were awarded tax-exempt status. Condoms, by contrast, would be subject to a 13 per cent tax from 2026. Families would no longer have to meet the cost of hospital childbirth (another disincentive to reproduce). Mass weddings and a much wider choice of matrimonial venues were encouraged to cut the cost of actually tying the knot within China. To conclude that all this was piecemeal and patchwork would hardly be unreasonable.

Conclusion

The first aspect of the United States and China from 2026 to 2049 to contemplate, therefore, is how different demography alone will make that second quarter of the twenty-first century diverge from the first. The two countries need to confront completely separate challenges.

For the United States it will be an evolving ethnic and racial composition which will mean that the proportion of white people will edge downwards year on year, the same will be true but less starkly for the black proportion of the American people, while the number of those who identify as Hispanic or Latinos, Asian-Americans and 'others' of multiple backgrounds will rise (and the average age of all of these sub-sets will be lower than that for white and black Americans).

There is clearly the risk of social tension in this transformation, but it has been occurring, steadily but slowly, for some decades. America as a whole will also become older, but its population will continue to rise and the number of those of working age will not collapse (and more of those who are older than sixty-five might voluntarily continue with full-time employment). This cannot truthfully be described as a demographic revolution. It is more evolutionary in nature.

For China, by contrast, the social change that is about to be encountered is more dramatic. A nation long used to having the largest population in the world will decrease in its size. Those who are there will become on average considerably older than they were a few decades ago. The ratio of the working-age population to those older than themselves will alter radically, quickly. This is a social revolution. It could be an economic one as well.

8

THE APPLES AND PEARS ECONOMIES

The economic transformation of China over the past four decades or so has been mesmerising. It intensified in the first decade of this century, as was showcased at the Beijing 2008 Olympic Games, itself the beneficiary of a $40 billion spending spree, a sum that was and remains unmatched by any other host city or nation. After a major economic stimulus introduced between 2009 and 2012 to avert any fall-out from the global financial crisis that had emanated from the United States, China was deploying more concrete than the US had used in the entire twentieth century. The country had more than 200 cities with at least a million people.

That sense of a remorseless drive forward continued into the next decade. China's total consumption in 2019 was still less than half that of the United States but growing very quickly. In 2021, total car sales in China were twenty-six million vehicles (compared with fifteen million in the US) and smartphone sales were 343 million (just 147 million in the US). China had become the world's largest producer of steel, solar panels, electronic goods, coal, plastics, electric vehicles and car batteries. Before the pandemic sent the shutters down, this surge in prosperity demonstrated itself in human manifestations. In 2019, Chinese outbound tourism spending had hit $255 billion with 155 million visits overseas. More than 700,000 Chinese students were studying in other countries. There were about 350 flights a week between China and the United States, overwhelmingly for business activities. All this in a nation where in living memory in the 1970s and 1980s, virtually no one knew anyone who had ever been abroad. It was mind-blowing.

It also created an almost Malthusian impulse to assume that everything would continue to move in that direction: that China would reliably register extraordinary annual growth rates, if not the 10 per cent or so that had been achieved in the early phases of its economic lift-off, perhaps an extension of the 7 per cent annual economic expansion that appeared to have become more or less a settled pattern in the 2000–2020 era. There was an enormous domestic consumer base that had only partially been tapped. Although there had been a dramatic shift in people from the countryside to the cities in barely two generations, there remained a sizeable rural population who could be encouraged to move towards the skyscrapers if the need for more labour existed.

On that basis there was, and to an extent continues to be, an excited argument about exactly when (not 'if' was the implication) the so-called 'crossover' would occur. At what point would the nominal GDP of China overtake that of the United States? Advocates of purchasing power parity would note that on that score, a crossover occurred at some point between 2016 and 2018. The overall size of GDP remains, however, the measurement that carries most weight.

This was a matter of interest to more than economists and statisticians. Those who occupied prominent positions in the

Chinese Communist Party had the metaphorical (perhaps actual) fireworks set to celebrate.

Their counterparts in Washington DC were no less fixated by the timing of this switch and how they would sell this as anything other than a de facto defeat inside the US and in the wider world.

At the height of this speculation, the hour of reckoning seemed to be drawing ever nearer. It would certainly occur at some point between 2026 and 2049. Serious analysts at the start of the 2010s deemed it plausible that the crossover might be witnessed in the earliest years of the second quarter of the twenty-first century, conceivably before 2030. Slightly more cautious and sober individuals and institutions mused that it might take a little longer but that it would be something of a shock if it did not materialise between 2030 and 2035.

While in a sense this was a numbers game, it undoubtedly had more than symbolic meaning. If there was anything likely to induce the Thucydides Trap that had been anticipated by Graham Allison, then it would be the sense that China's economy was leaving that of the US in its wake. Who would want to be US President, Treasury Secretary or Chairman of the Fed on that day?

When exactly that day might be now looks rather more uncertain. Matters appear somewhat different now than they did at the start of the 2020s just before Covid-19 surfaced. Many of the organisations which had asserted that the crossover would occur before the decade was out, to be followed by a rampant 2030s when China quickly established a dominant GDP lead over the United States, have had to refine their stance somewhat. In some cases, this involved caveats. In others there has been a climbdown. Few would now argue with any certainty that the US will lose its leadership in the global GDP ranking during President Trump's second term or shortly afterwards. Even those who had suggested that it might be the early 2030s have softened that stance.

The date for the crossover has edged back to the late 2030s, possibly the early 2040s. It is no longer outrageous to suggest that it might not be seen even in 2049, such is the uncertainty.

This reassessment has been triggered by several factors. At least ten of them are worth listing.

The US and Chinese economies are fundamentally different

This is not a comparison between two economies that are essentially similar, with a more established one and an upstart competitor. They are fundamentally different. The United States has an economy that is fully developed, driven by (primarily) domestic consumption, framed by innovation, service-orientated and extraordinary in its scale and its international reach. China, on the other hand, is still in essence a developing country (with no guarantee that it will at any point become as fully developed as the American model), which relies disproportionately on the export of manufactured goods and thus the ebbs and flows of international trade, and retains an extremely large array of state-owned enterprises. These are apples and pears.

That can be seen by looking more forensically at the headline GDP numbers. In 2024, the estimate for US GDP placed it at $29,167 billion. China's GDP came in at $18,273 billion. Put another way, the United States was responsible for 26.3 per cent of global GDP, with China second at 16.9 per cent (which made the two nations together a staggering 43.2 per cent of

Planet Earth's economy). The American economy is, therefore, about 1.6 times the size of China's. Quite a margin.

The overall GDP figures, furthermore, mask a more significant story. GDP per head in the US exceeds $80,000. GDP per head in China does not yet touch $15,000. In per capita income terms this means that the average American is more than five times wealthier than the typical Chinese citizen. The United States is the sixth- or seventh-richest country in the world in GDP per capita. China, despite its huge advances, is the seventieth-richest. Once again, apples and pears.

Only niche microstates and the oil-producing countries of the Gulf are, in per capita terms, more prosperous than America. It has the highest median household income in the OECD. Those who live in its poorest state – Mississippi – are better off than they would be if they were British or Canadian and very close to (possibly even very slightly ahead of) where they would be if they were German. The division between the really well-off states of the North-East and California (despite its recent challenges) and Western Europe is just enormous. The gap between these regions and almost anywhere in China is a chasm. Apples and pears.

The underlying strength of the American economy should never be forgotten. It is the world's largest importer and (although it is quite a modest percentage of GDP) the second-largest exporter. It has the world's largest consumer market in terms of purchasing capacity. Walmart, which operates primarily within the United States, is the world's largest company and also the biggest private sector employer on the planet. It has 2.1 million employees overall, two-thirds of whom are based in America. There is no business in either China or in Europe that is close to it.

Finally, the hard fundamentals. New York City is the financial capital of the world and has been for approximately a century since it eclipsed London. Even though manufacturing is less than a fifth of its economy, the US is still the second-largest manufacturer out there (after China). It is the world's most substantial producer of petroleum and natural gas. It has in the dollar what is without doubt the world's reserve currency. It has the largest stockpile of gold in the world (at more than 8,000 tonnes). It does not actually need to be notionally the largest economy in GDP terms in order to retain any of the above advantages. It would still be one of a kind.

The performance of the American economy is, if anything, improving

It might have appeared initially that it was the United States that had been hit for six by the pandemic as it struggled to muster a coherent response to Covid-19 and succumbed to a sharp recession as a result of it. In reality, the bounce-back has been exceptional. It has meant that, again employing nominal GDP (measured by market exchange rates), the US not only stayed significantly larger as an economy than China between 2020 and 2025, its advantage widened by no less than $10 trillion during this period. Some of this has been due to the depreciation of the Chinese currency against the dollar, but that decline is in itself revealing. This meant that in comparative terms, China's GDP actually shrank vis-à-vis the United States, from being close to three-quarters of its size to a figure much nearer to two-thirds. This was not widely predicted.

It is also part of a longer-run trend that has not received sufficient attention. In the early 1990s, in part prompted by a deep recession, pessimism about the American economy was pervasive. It was mistaken. From 1993 onwards, the United

States motored with a few short outings to the pit lane. It constituted about 40 per cent of G7 GDP in 1990. By 2025 it was verging on 50 per cent of it. That shift in gear has become even more forceful recently. The American economy expanded by 10 per cent between 2020 and 2025, three times more than the rest of the G7 managed. There was an almost unanimous view among economists in 2023 that a recession was at hand. Growth in excess of 3 per cent actually materialised. The United Kingdom, to make a comparison, has seen growth at that level (apart from that which occurred when the first Covid-19 lockdown ended) only once in any year since the global financial crisis which struck it and the globe fifteen plus years ago.

In economic terms, it is thus very taxing to make the argument that the United States is in decline. Quite the opposite. It will not notch up the growth rates of China from 2000 to 2020 because it is not a developing country that is starting from a very low base. It is mature. The dilemma for China is that it is not a developing country starting from a very low base anymore. But it is not yet mature. It may have been through economic puberty but that is fast ending. It will unavoidably become harder and harder to replicate the growth rates of 2010–2020, never mind the astronomical figures achieved in 2000–2010. The 2020s are a much harder slog.

The private sector is America's blessing, while the public sector is China's curse

There are many structural differences between the economies of the United States and China but one of the most profound is the comparative size of the private and public sectors. The private sector is responsible for 85 per cent of the American economy, and a large slice of the 15 per cent that falls under the public sector is military expenditure. The country has thirty million small businesses. Although the biggest brand names may be the largest employers, it is more modest companies that fuel the stark majority of employment creation, especially when times are good. This is also a private sector that operates with relatively few external restrictions imposed on it. Hiring and firing in the US is much more straightforward than in Europe and aspiring employees are much more willing to be geographically mobile than would be expected of Europeans. This comes with its downsides. The country does not legally guarantee its workers paid vacations or sick days, although most employers will offer these as benefits, nor is paid parental leave a legal right (placing the US with Papua New Guinea, Suriname and Liberia in this regard). To offset this, however, US workers, on average, can earn significantly higher wages than their British and European counterparts.

If the private sector is America's blessing, then the public sector is China's curse. At the height of its advance (around 2005–2015), the private sector accounted for almost 65 per cent of the economy overall. Then official attitudes towards it changed. In short order it has retreated back to about 40 per cent.

There has been a substantial efficiency loss as a consequence. China has sought to promote a private sector ethos within its many state-owned enterprises but has not made much progress. There is a critical cultural difference to existing, living and possibly failing in a market context. The incentives and inducements for state-owned enterprises are not the same. Decisions are taken for reasons other than supply and demand. All too often, the 'P' in the 'P&L' will stand not for profit but for politics.

This is hardly a secret. As Kevin Rudd, the former Australian Prime Minister and a sympathetic expert on China, has asserted: 'Most economists' evaluation of the reasons for this [economic underperformance] is clear: the continued size, influence and unproductive investment of the state sector.' Those at the sharp end within China appreciate this too. Although not a politically popular call, the Central Economic Work Conference in 2023 openly asked for 'unwavering deepening reform' and 'unswervingly expanding openness'. When it comes to cutting back and closing down the deadweight state-owned enterprises, they are probably going to be disappointed.

China has a serious youth unemployment and underemployment issue

Before its seemingly remorseless rise was restrained and restricted, the private sector in China performed an additional service to the economy. It was the overwhelming force for the growth of employment, particularly for younger citizens and especially for those who had just graduated.

This was of real importance because the number of these highly educated individuals had increased sharply, and their expectations of the world of work and their place in it were high. At one stage it was estimated that the private sector was responsible for up to nine in ten of new employment opportunities.

The situation today and for the immediate future, perhaps beyond, is quite different. China has youth unemployment in the range of 16–18 per cent (the numbers have become so embarrassing that the authorities have sought to suppress them) and, even more significantly, what may be termed youth underemployment (graduates feeling forced to take up roles rather less attractive than they might have anticipated) may well be in the range of 16–18 per cent as well.

Furthermore, the number of graduates emerging in the first part of the second quarter of this century will continue to increase (even as the overall proportion of younger people in the whole population falls). Finding suitable positions anywhere other than a revitalised private sector looks like an extremely tall order. Yet social and ultimately political contentment relies on it.

The productivity problem

Much of what has been established so far comes down to differences in productivity. Economic growth can be obtained by bringing more people at the same level of productivity into an economy and/or by ensuring that those people are more productive than they were previously.

This can be encouraged by capital investment that improves output per head, or by reducing the costs of the economic activity involved or enhancing the skills of those involved. With its working-age population having already peaked, the option of simply throwing more people at the economy is no longer there for China. The United States could, if it so desired, throw open its doors and substantially increase its population through immigration far more easily than China, but it is unlikely that its electorate would cheer on what would probably be seen as competition, even if immigration is less of a political taboo in capitalist America than in communist China.

With what economists usually regard as the benign magic wand of mass immigration absent, there is not much else that can be done other than induce much higher levels of productivity.

The United States has proved spectacularly effective at doing this and over a sustained length of time. It has seen a 70 per cent increase in productivity since 1990, compared with 29 per cent in Europe and 25 per cent in Japan. This means that output per head in the US is about 30 per cent higher than in Europe and Canada and 60 per cent more than in Japan. This has been the trigger for leaving the G7 in the dust.

If China is brought into the frame, then the productivity problem becomes even more relevant. Despite the incredible increase in the overall size of its economy, output per head in China is less than a third of that witnessed in the United States. This fact alone almost cancels out the advantage that China should have in holding a very much larger population overall than the US.

The differences between the two economies in the role of their private and public sectors are a crucial element here. A comparison between the two private sectors would be less flattering to the United States and there are areas where it might well be placed second to China. However, these differences are not the only factor at work. While looking at the two private sectors alone would be less cheering for the US, it still, on the whole, has a tangible advantage overall.

This is due to innovation and to capital investment. By the standards of larger developed economies, what really makes the United States stand out from the crowd is the scale of its research and development initiatives. At almost 3.5 per cent of GDP, it is the leader of the pack. It is only beaten by smaller and relatively boutique economies such as that of Israel. China has made strides in this area and has probably reached R&D expenditure of about 2.5 per cent of GDP. The quality as well as the quantity of American spending here is, though, very often far superior.

Energy sufficiency

The age when the American economy appeared to be in most difficulty, even decline, was the 1970s, although few countries other than Japan and to a degree West Germany had much to enjoy in the course of that decade. The drain on the United States was that its economy depended on oil, and it had to import an extremely sizeable proportion of it from the Middle East, which made it politically exposed to what was a volatile region at the best of times and a reluctant client of OPEC. Sharp movements in oil prices induced recessions in 1973–1974 and 1979–1980 and also had some responsibility for the slowdown in 1991–1992, the last time that an oil price shock could really be cited as the explanation for the US finding itself in economic troubles. If that dependency had continued, then it is hard to conceive how the country could have made the unanticipated progress that it has over the past thirty years.

The salvation of the United States has been the discovery and exploitation of shale oil. It still requires some imports from the Middle East for certain sorts of high-quality oil but much of what it needs on a day-to-day basis can now be found domestically. Shale oil is also comparatively cheap to extract, certainly when compared with acquiring oil via deepwater drilling. There are undoubtedly environmental side-effects, but in most places where the finest finds of shale have occurred it has been possible to extract it without significant public opposition. This tends to be most true when it is the Republican

Party that holds sway in Washington. The words 'drill, baby, drill' have rarely been far from Donald Trump's lips on the campaign trail or in public comments since he returned to the White House in January 2025. To emphasise the point, they were inserted in capital letters in the Republican Party platform endorsed by the national convention in July 2024. This 'liquid gold', as Mr Trump described it in his inauguration address, has been at the heart of the new US economy.

The impact has been transformative. The United States now produces some thirteen million barrels of crude oil per day and three billion cubic metres per day of natural gas. Such a result would have been unimaginable in the 1970s. It has become the world's largest producer of oil and gas. It has an energy surplus of $65 billion annually. A full tenth of all the expansion of the American economy between 2020 and 2025 was the direct result of additional energy extraction. What is more, all of these figures are likely to be higher, perhaps much higher, by 2030.

China has no such reservoir of liquid gold. It will continue to be an importer of both oil and gas.

Stock market supremacy

When it comes to stock markets the United States is a superpower with scarcely any competition. The New York Stock Exchange and Nasdaq are utterly dominant. This is not merely a boon for those fortunate enough to work in high finance, it has an effect on the wider economy too. Overseas companies are drawn to the United States to list there. It has been the consistent complaint of venture capital in Europe that once the new and desirable businesses that they have backed reach a certain scale, then it is on Nasdaq that they want to be floated.

The size of the American edge here is stunning. In terms of the totality of global stock market valuation, the United States is responsible for 61 per cent, the rest of the world bar China for 36.2 per cent and China itself a humble 2.8 per cent. The notion that Shanghai is poised to do to New York City in the 2020s what New York did to London in the 1920s is surreal. There is no contest to speak of.

That 60+ per cent number is almost as high as the historical American peak in the 1960s. It is actually more astonishing because there were far fewer stock markets then and stocks and shares did not play the role in individual and institutional prosperity that they do today.

It is in the technology sphere that the American advantage is at its mightiest. The seven biggest US tech firms – the 'Magnificent Seven' (namely Alphabet, Amazon, Apple, Meta, Microsoft, Nvidia and Tesla) – are together worth more than the whole stock markets of Britain, China and Germany. This is a source of capital that is a gigantic asset not only to those firms but to the United States as an economic powerhouse. There is no chance of China outflanking them.

Foreign direct investment

Foreign direct investment (FDI) is both an inflow of capital to the economy of a country and a vote of confidence (or not) in that economy and country. The United States has invariably been both the largest recipient of FDI and the biggest source of it. There was a period, from 2010 to 2020, when China appeared to be well set to challenge its supremacy. Foreign investors were flocking into the country to place what appeared to be one-way bets across a variety of sectors. In retrospect, there was a dangerous herd mentality emerging. It was becoming the Wild East.

When such sentiment turns, it can do so with extraordinary ferocity. The herd is entirely capable of turning as one and storming off in a different direction. There can be official influence at work here: the words 'America First' do not require much interpretation in US boardrooms. Yet it was not the Trump Effect but the Xi Effect that led not only American investors but those located in Europe, the Middle East and other sections of East Asia to decide to put their cash elsewhere. China was seen to have soured on the private sector, and as this was the only element of the economy in which outsiders would want to take a stake, that was a serious disincentive. Added to this, legislative and regulatory change made investors increasingly anxious that while they may be able to get their money in, they were unclear about what might happen next and how to get it out again.

This means that the most recent distribution of foreign direct investment is telling. The US in 2024 received 23.7 per cent of it (comfortably the most substantial sum for any country), while the rest of the world bar China attracted 67.7 per cent. China declined to 8.6 per cent (it had been 21.1 per cent in 2011). This is more than slippage. It is an outright slump. It is hard to regain confidence once it is forfeited.

The dangers of debt

Outsiders have also become much more acutely aware of the level of debt within China and this has also ended the era of euphoria about its economy. China has a debt ratio to GDP of about 300 per cent, a percentage that has basically doubled since 2008. The United States has a ratio which, although historically high, is about one-third of that figure. Many assumed that a soaring debt ratio in China was the by-product of an astounding age of expansion and would start to settle down and then reverse itself as the economy became more developed. This looks mistaken.

It is not easy to stem the flow of debt without heavy-handed official intervention. When it has been introduced, it has often been counterproductive. Fiscal policy in China is rather wayward. The tax base is chaotic in that less than a tenth of the population is estimated to contribute to income tax at all and even the super-rich seem able to order their affairs so that they can avoid it. As a result, sales taxes (inherently regressive) count for almost 40 per cent of the total take.

Local government collects most of the other taxation that exists and also controls nearly 90 per cent of total government expenditure. Central government might think that it is able to ordain what is spent by Party and local officials, but in practice it is often a game of cat-and-mouse.

How much debt is too much debt? No one really knows and no one wants to find out the limit. If there were to be a crisis then, unlike in the United States, where in the event of any kind of default, overseas institutions would feel much of the anguish too, in China, a high savings ratio and a largely closed capital account mean that almost 95 per cent of China's debt is domestic in its orientation. If there is a level (325 per cent? 350 per cent? 400 per cent?) at which everything comes crashing down, then the whole of the economy will, in virtual isolation, have to absorb the entire hit. This is not a subject that any member of the Standing Committee of the Politburo would wish to make public comment on. A few more independent figures have, rather bravely, done so. They include Xiang Songzuo, Professor of Economics at the People's University in Beijing, who has stated candidly, 'China's economy is all built on speculation, and everything is overleveraged.'

Perils of property

It does not take much in the way of detective work to identify where in the system a timebomb might be ticking. It lies in a mania for property that the authorities lost command over (if they ever had much authority in this realm in the first place). It is located at the interconnection between the banking system and those engaged in the buying and selling of housing across the country.

A few numbers indicate why there is peril here. As of the end of 2020, the property sector represented 29 per cent of Chinese GDP, 41 per cent of all bank loans and 78 per cent of the wealth that had been invested by urban Chinese. These figures have not shifted much since. The potential for a catastrophe here is obvious. A huge number of houses have been built for which there was no real demand and so they cannot be sold at anything like the price anticipated. It has been suggested that there is nearly enough empty property in China to house the entire population of Germany. Added to which, according to *The Economist* in September 2024, some twenty to thirty million households are thought to have paid for houses that have never been completed. When it becomes clear that their savings are not coming back to them, there will be some very angry citizens who want compensation from someone. China may yet endure its own variation of the financial crisis that struck the US in 2008/2009.

The crossover conundrum

It is now clear why the crossover date at which the United States and China exchange places as the first- and second-largest economies by nominal GDP has been, to put it mildly, reconsidered. The original predictions consistently underestimated the continuing force of the US economy and overestimated the extent to which China could continue to grow by levels of 6–7 per cent without the risk of coming off the rails. The United States is not an economy that is in decline. It has shown the capacity to renew itself yet again. If the costs of energy become cheaper and it continues to be the earliest adopter of new ideas and technologies, then it will not be eclipsed easily. It has assets that no other nation has ever enjoyed. They will carry on through the 2020s and after.

China has much to say for it as well. It has witnessed an astounding surge but is at risk of encountering the 'middle income trap'. This is a concept first devised by the economists Indermit Singh Gill and Homi Kharas in 2007 to describe economies which after a burst of growth find they are squeezed between low-wage competitors and rich-country innovators. China could yet pivot and maintain its momentum, but a dead-hand public sector will not do it. The approach to economic policy that has been adopted in recent years may prove a liability. If it does not shift stance, then the crossover may move ever further into the distance. It may even, as George Magnus, Research Associate at the China Centre at Oxford University and a former chief economist at SG Warburg and UBS, has openly mused, never come to pass at all.

9

ARMY DREAMERS

> The risks and challenges we face have obviously increased. It is unrealistic to always want a peaceful life and not want to fight. [We] need to disregard wishful thinking, be brave to fight and refuse to give way even one inch of matters of principle. We need to safeguard our nation's sovereignty, security and development interests with unprecedented will and character.
>
> Xi Jinping, Central Party School, 1 September 2021

The above statement, made in a public forum, will strike many who read it as unwelcome and close to extraordinary. It would seem to suggest that not only is the Chinese leader prepared for the idea of an outright conflict with the United States, he is all but resigned to it. It fits a pattern of mutual hostility that has become a default position in certain circles. Nor is it limited to China.

A substantial section of the US Republican Party believes that China is not just a strategic rival to the United States, it is essentially an enemy. The decks must be cleared of all other considerations in US foreign policy thinking. To place weight on almost anything else that might happen elsewhere is a delusional distraction. Michael Waltz, for instance, the ultimately short-lived first National Security Advisor to President Trump in his second term, insisted in early 2025 that both the Russian invasion of Ukraine and the Israeli incursion into the Gaza Strip in response to the appalling attack on its people in 2023 were matters that should be got out of the way as swiftly as possible by the new administration, so that it could focus on what really mattered: the menace that the Chinese Communist Party represented to the security of the USA.

To take these words literally is to assume that the forces that are pushing the United States and China in the direction of conflict, as Graham Allison insisted in 2017 was indeed the case, are so overwhelming that almost nothing exists that can resist them. Is this really a matter of when, not if?

The relationship between the United States and China is and will be central to the international order in the years to come. That is where the consensus ends. Predictions and expectations about how the two nations will manage their perhaps inevitable rivalry vary enormously. Recent events and statements have led to increasing debate over a direct or 'hot' conflict between the powers in the context of Taiwan, while others have asserted that an overt clash between the US and China is unlikely, but something akin to the Cold War involving the US and the USSR in the forty-five or so years after 1945 is highly conceivable. Another school of thought, one that has received less attention of late, is that the notion of a military confrontation – be it 'hot' or 'cold' – is essentially a distraction from the real nature of their contest, which is economic and, fundamentally, technological.

The 'hot war' thesis

The notion of a 'hot war' between the United States and China, once deemed improbable, has had a high-profile airing. This has in part been because certain US military figures have mused publicly about the possibility (including one General who opined in 2023 that it was his 'gut feeling' that the US and China would be engaged in fighting in Taiwan by 2025), reports that President Xi Jinping had told the Chinese military 'to be ready to invade Taiwan by 2027' (although an alternative translation of what he had allegedly asserted is that China should 'be capable of' launching an assault by 2027, a subtly different message) and the self-evident tension between Washington and Beijing over the flight of a super-sized balloon in February 2023 containing spying equipment, which led, for a time, to an utterly glacial bilateral relationship, and Chinese arms supplies to Russia which would be used in Ukraine. All of this prompted even the normally cautious magazine *The Economist* to highlight the threat of war.

The more sober critique that provides the basis for the 'hot war' argument is as follows. China, it is said, has a limited window of opportunity in the second half of this decade during which it will have the military capacity to mount a full-scale invasion of what it sees as a 'renegade province', before Taiwan acquires the ability to see off such an attack by its own rearmament. The reunification of China is sufficiently important to its leadership, this contention runs, that it will act in the approximately five-year opening (2026–2031) that it has available to it, even if this runs the risk of not only air and sea military engagement with the US but a land clash on Taiwanese soil too. Everything that China is doing in terms of the build-up of its armed forces is framed in this context.

The open wound

To those living outside the region, the fixation, even obsession, that Beijing has with Taiwan borders on the incomprehensible, especially in the light of the advances that China itself has made over the past forty years. It is a comparatively small island (strictly speaking a collection of 168 islands, but most of them are little more than rocks) of some strategic significance, but not to such an extent that it would seem worth the energy that the CCP has expended in seeking to isolate it internationally nor the degree to which military spending and activity have been skewed towards the Taiwan theatre, especially when that involves a significant opportunity cost elsewhere.

The symbolism of Taiwan to mainland China (and by no means only those at the top of the CCP) should not be underestimated. The island was undoubtedly part of imperial China historically, its population is overwhelmingly ethnically Chinese, and its culture cannot be separated from that of China. For a civilisation state like China that has suffered division, invasion and disunion for centuries, that Taiwan is the last part of the national jigsaw puzzle yet to be completed is very painful. Were it to be reincorporated, there would be a sense that China was whole again. It would be an outcome that eluded Mao Zedong despite the argument made (by his supporters) that all of his other sins are essentially washed clean by the fact that he restored unity and sovereignty after a century when a succession of outsiders ravaged China, often with brutality. That Taiwan is not in China and, worse, conspicuously does not want to be, is an open wound.

Politics as well as emotion are in play. Events in Taiwan have long been an irritation to Beijing. In the 1960s, the island experienced an economic miracle at exactly the same time as the mainland sank into an economic and social abyss through the Great Leap Forward and then the Cultural Revolution. China had thought of Taiwan as backward. It was being overtaken by it despite the vast disparity in the population sizes of the two places. The success of Hong Kong under UK rule was almost as annoying. The CCP could, nonetheless, at least take comfort from its success in unseating Taiwan in the UN and through it obtaining a permanent seat on the UN Security Council. That Taiwan managed, thanks to its US patron, to cling on to that elevated status, despite a laughable claim to be the sole 'real' government of all China now, looks like an *Alice in Wonderland* arrangement, but it lasted twenty-two years.

Any warm glow felt by the Chinese leadership did not last long. Taiwan then managed with considerable flair to transition peacefully from an authoritarian state, which habitually insisted that the threat posed by China meant it could not afford debate and division, into a lively, viable, multi-party democracy with commendably free and fair presidential and parliamentary elections from 1996 onwards. If that were possible in one section of the Chinese sphere, why not in China itself?

Taiwan had therefore become a developed economy, a thriving civil society and a poster child for democratic transitions. If this did not aggrieve the rulers in Beijing enough, Taiwan was increasingly inclined to vote for the 'wrong' side. Its system was just about tolerable when it returned the Kuomintang to office. That Party acknowledged the broad principle of 'One China' even if it showed few signs of wanting to rush back into the clutches of the mainland. A business understanding could be struck and trade encouraged, and family visits between relatives who had been separated in 1949 could be offered within this arrangement. There might have been an element of fiction and farce in all of this but that was mutually convenient. It suited Xi Jinping's predecessors to play along.

In recent years, and most relevantly for the majority of the time that Xi Jinping has been at the helm, the electorate of Taiwan has been less accommodating. Tsai Ing-wen, a charismatic female figure who was the nominee of the Democratic Progressive Party (DPP), won the presidency in 2016 by a landslide and her Party was well entrenched in Parliament after the ballots were counted there. She and her associates were re-elected four years later. Even more infuriatingly, despite China making it manifest how much Beijing disapproved of him, the DPP contender Lai Ching-te captured the presidency in 2024, albeit chiefly courtesy of a split in the opposition vote.

In all of this, China and Xi had a sense that the United States was stirring the pot. Under the first Trump administration, the American fleet was more visible in the waters around Taiwan and arms sales increased as Taiwan sought to modernise its own military much as China had already done. There was a combined exercise between American and Taiwanese troops for the first time in forty years. A steady stream of (initially low-level) US officials started to visit the island. In August 2020, Alex Azar, the American Health and Human Services Secretary, became the highest-ranking US figure to be seen in Taiwan for four decades. An Undersecretary of State came a month later. Shortly afterwards, Kelly Craft, the US Ambassador to the UN, met with Taiwan's top official in New York City. Beijing could hardly contain its fury at what it saw as a breach of the US 'One China' dictum.

That rage if anything intensified after Mr Trump had made way for Mr Biden. The visit of Nancy Pelosi, then the Democratic Speaker of the House of Representatives, clearly acting with the consent of the White House, in August 2022 caused a political coronary in Beijing and vigorous sabre-rattling. What, if anything, could China do about a Taiwan that enrages it?

Taking out Taiwan

Even allowing for the further advance of the Chinese military over the next few years, the task of invading and then occupying Taiwan (rather than simply seeking to obliterate it) is an incredibly challenging one. The practical constraints are considerable and essentially render the notion of a swift and surgical strike something close to inconceivable.

The first such constraint is the sheer distance involved. At its narrowest point, the Taiwan Strait is 128 kilometres (79.5 miles) wide, itself a sizeable distance to travel. When realistic embarkation and disembarkation points are taken into account, the sea voyage required becomes at least 50 per cent longer still. The notion that an invasion could be conceived secretly or by stealth lacks any kind of credibility.

The preparation required for such an undertaking would be huge and involve many months of planning and moving the relevant supplies into position. It would be close to impossible to avoid such activity being detected in advance, with Taiwan and its allies able to anticipate what might be directed at them. The idea that it would be viable to disguise all or part of this war effort as a 'military exercise' verges upon the ludicrous. It would need to be the longest 'military exercise' ever recorded. Real intentions would be signalled.

The waters concerned include numerous well-fortified islands between China and Taiwan that are home to an array of extremely effective surveillance and early warning facilities which would enable an attack to be observed and obstructed well before Taiwan itself was struck. The odds of orchestrating an attack that had a genuine sense of surprise are about zero.

Any actual invasion would require a vast and slow-moving fleet transporting a minimum of 300,000 troops (more plausibly double or triple that number). The force would have to be much larger still if it were not possible to use the facilities at ports captured largely intact in Taiwan in order to ensure the necessary supply lines back to mainland China. This creates the paradox that destroying key Taiwanese assets would complicate any military incursion.

Taiwan has few beaches (a maximum of fourteen) that would be suitable for amphibious landings to allow incoming troops to establish a viable base on the island.

Taiwan also has an unusual topography which affords it additional security. It has a heavily forested mountain ridge which runs down almost the whole length of the eastern side of the island for 395 kilometres (245 miles). Cities are spread out around this ridge in a fashion that is close to a natural defensive barrier. This makes conquest of the entire territory exceptionally difficult and would probably require intense, street-by-street urban warfare, of which the People's Liberation Army has no experience whatsoever, while the defenders of this terrain, albeit outnumbered, would have the seminal asset of detailed local knowledge.

Taiwan has developed its own state-of-the-art offensive weapons. It has an impressive air force which can operate using tunnels cut into mountains and is supplemented by its own satellite systems and ultra-sensitive radar. Controlling the skies over the island by knocking out the Taiwanese air defence system would be an exceptionally ambitious endeavour.

All the above assumes that Taiwan is on its own in a confrontation with China. It is more probable that the United States, and even Japan, might feel compelled to intervene in a war. When a new Japanese Prime Minister, Sanae Takaichi, publicly acknowledged this possibility in 2025, the response of the authorities in Beijing was fury and a boycott of Chinese tourism to Japan.

This would hardly be President Trump's own preference. Left to his own devices he might conclude that Taiwan was neither his nor his country's fight. If compelled to do something he might want to opt for comprehensive sanctions, a suspension of diplomatic ties and another round of tariffs.

It is doubtful that he could sustain a stand of indifference. His Vice President, Secretary of State and Secretary of Defense would be up in arms. The Senate would pass resolutions urging a response. Much of the Republican Party would demand that he ensure that Taiwan was not overrun. The Democrats, even if they were motivated mainly by opportunism, would cast him as a weakling. The media would be on his back as well. He would soon find himself surrounded. Nor is it plausible that the Chinese would seize Taiwan at such speed that anyone around the President could assert that, very sadly, it was simply too late for any US intervention to be contemplated. Besides which, it cannot be said that the Commander-in-Chief would lack the resources to act should they be called upon.

The American presence in this part of the Pacific Ocean is stunning. The US Seventh Fleet is located at Okinawa, Japan. This facility contains thirty-two separate bases, a large air fleet, 20,000+ US Marines, at least one aircraft carrier strike group (and often two of them) and several cruise missile submarines. This by itself is a formidable armada and one which China would have to assume would respond. If Japan were to enter the strife, the fourth-largest navy in the world would also be engaged in Taiwan. Outside the wayward North Korean regime, China could rely on few regional allies of any value to it.

The cost of conflict

The cost of a conflict, while obviously transformational for Taiwan, would be staggering for China.

Military losses would be massive and a seismic shock for a country that has not been in a significant conflict since it raided Vietnam in 1979 (and was forced back behind its borders). The danger of outright dissent against the Communist Party leadership would be sizeable.

The economic fall-out would be on an epic scale. The best estimates are that China's GDP would rapidly shrink by between a quarter and a third. This is without the full impact of sanctions against its exports which would surely result from any invasion.

The diplomatic and reputational damage to China as it aspires to present itself as a crucial player in global politics would be ruinous. The costs of a conflict far outweigh any benefits. That would remain true even if Taiwan could be totally subdued (which is itself doubtful).

The 'tepid war' option

China does not need the complexity, cost or chaos of a war to achieve its minimum objectives as they concern Taiwan. Avoiding such a situation has become even more appealing in the light of the disaster that the Russian attempt to subjugate Ukraine has proved for Moscow and its ruling elites.

What China wants above all else is to avoid Taiwan formally declaring its independence and for the United States then to recognise its autonomy. There is a range of military options open to Beijing that would fall well short of a 'hot war' but nonetheless act as a strong disincentive for any President and government of Taiwan to claim independence. China could seize some of the outlying islands between its coastline and that of Taiwan. It could substantially increase its flights into the airspace which Taiwan considers to be its own. It might, if it wanted to take matters further, blockade ports. A 'tepid war' of this form would be enough to convince most in Taiwan to stick with the status quo.

This appears set to be the pattern in the region. An unusually large arms sale in 2025 by the restored Trump Oval Office was swiftly followed by a series of military drills by China – 'Justice Mission 2025' – involving eighty-nine military aircraft, twenty-eight warships and a set of coastguard vessels. Taiwan took this in its stride.

A new 'cold war' instead?

If a 'hot war' is avoidable, then the idea that we are heading for a repeat of the old Cold War might have an enticing logic to it. The term 'Cold War' is, at one level, flexible enough to cover any variety of antagonism that might be witnessed between the United States and China. Yet if it is to imply an international system broadly the same as that of the US and the Soviet Union, then it is badly flawed.

The distinctive features of the Cold War (a term put in the public domain by George Orwell in 1945) include the following three conditions:

- a contest of belief systems (capitalism versus communism as social structures);
- a struggle between superpowers both of which had achieved truly global military reach;
- the mutual possibility of absolute nuclear annihilation by either side of the other.

Where the world is now – and likely to be for an extended period – is different to this.

Contest of systems?

The US–China relationship is not a clash of belief systems. In both countries, nationalism is a more important factor than was true of the US–USSR era. Washington is more likely to talk in terms of 'American values' than the virtues of capitalism as such, and free market idealism is not what it once was (especially inside the Republican Party which has strayed from the Reagan model). China's notion of 'market socialism' (with a lively internal argument about the balance between the 'market' and the 'socialism' aspects of it, currently moving away from the former to the latter) is not really being offered or presented as an export to other countries. Indeed, the consistent aspect of the Chinese Communist Party's outlook is an emphasis on the vital 'Chinese characteristics' of its methodology. Whereas Soviet Communism regarded itself as something with universal qualities ripe to be adopted across the planet,

China tends to stress the unique elements of its political approach.

Global reach?

It is in terms of 'global reach', however, that any concept of a Cold War II falls apart. The US has a global reach in military terms. China is still striving to secure regional authority in its neighbourhood.

This can be seen in a few basic comparisons between the military capacities of the two countries.

While China's spending on defence has increased markedly over the past twenty years and as a percentage of GDP outstrips the US, in absolute dollar terms (at about $250 billion) it is still well less than a third that of the current United States military budget (at above $960 billion and rising). For context, although exact comparisons are challenging, the US in the second Trump term appears to be spending more in simple cash than the next ten nations combined (China, Russia, Germany, the UK, India, Saudi Arabia, Japan, Ukraine, France and South Korea). By the time that Mr Trump leaves office it could increase to a size that means it has eclipsed Italy and Israel (possibly Poland) as well.

Although China is often described as having 'the largest navy in the world', which it does, strictly speaking (about 332 vessels to 291 for the United States according to the Pentagon), the statistic is misleading. Having lots and lots of comparatively small boats does not constitute a 'global reach'. It is far better to have a smaller number of larger ships to realise that end. China has two aircraft carriers (with three more under construction and three more planned by 2035). The United States Navy has eleven of them, with two more near completion and an additional seven in the pipeline. The existing carriers contain an average of around eighty fighters (the largest in the world) and they have a total combined deck space that is over twice as large as that of all other nations combined. The US can supplement this astonishing armada with nine helicopter carriers (China has three, comparatively small, such vessels). China has acquired many more submarines but most of these are designed for the conditions of the relatively shallow South China Sea and would be of limited value in deeper waters far from China's mainland.

In terms of overall tonnage (2023 figures), the US ranks first with some 4.5 million tonnes. China comes in second with a relatively modest two million tonnes. There is simply no competition here in terms of real global power. All of this will be reinforced robustly by the Australia–UK–US (or AUKUS) security alliance sealed under the Biden administration which will allow Australia, in particular, to play a critical supporting role in the Pacific Ocean, to China's deep disapproval.

It is a similar story and ratio when it comes to combat aircraft. The US has more than twice as many of these as China, with technological superiority and finer pilots. The US Air Force also has assets with a much longer range than those of China and which could operate with a much greater firepower.

Only when it comes to the armies of the two countries does China (superficially) have a lead. The People's Liberation Army is approximately 975,000 individuals strong, more than twice the size of the regular US Army (about 480,000 persons). The difference, though, is that 99 per cent of the PLA is located within China, responsible for 22,117 km (13,743 miles) of borders with fourteen nations. The United States Armed Forces (the Army plus other services) are everywhere.

Everywhere really means everywhere. It is the wide disparity between the US and China in terms of overseas bases that delivers the fatal blow to any Cold War comparison. The United States has at least 750 bases internationally. China has, depending on what you regard as an overseas base, one, two, three, five or eight such bases. Why the uncertainty?

The only absolutely unambiguous Chinese overseas base is in Djibouti in the Horn of Africa. Beijing is supposedly erecting a building at the Ream base in Cambodia on a twenty-five-year lease but its exact nature remains unknown (and the Americans have an outpost at the same place anyway). Some sort of construction is also occurring in Tajikistan but so close to the Chinese border that it is rather stretching the idea of an overseas base to its limits. There are five other (small) examples of China having created man-made bases in either disputed or international waters close to its own coastline. If you just count the ones that most neutrals would agree were not Chinese territory, the overall number of 'overseas' bases is five. Accept all of them as outside China, then it is eight. Any attempt to equate US–China today with the old US–USSR era starts to look surreal.

Furthermore, this is not a competition in which one could expect China to 'catch up' swiftly. To be of any serious utility, an overseas base needs to be one where (a) there is a stable and sympathetic host country and regime and (b) a place of significant strategic significance, and (c) where the location fulfils a military need (so deep-water ports for a navy to be located). The supply of such assets internationally is finite, and the US already has the pick of the planet.

Nuclear equivalence?

Finally, in terms of the crude currency that is nuclear weapons and the prospect of Armageddon, this is not the Cold War

Revisited either. The US holds, according to the most recently available data, a stockpile of 6,000 nuclear weapons of which 1,650 are actively deployed (on a missile so ready to go if required). China has between 350 and 400 in total, most of which are submarine-based, so perhaps about half of them are actively deployed (and with a much more limited range than their US counterparts). On a day-to-day basis, France, with 280 actively deployed nuclear weapons, commands a bigger arsenal.

A cold peace?

Whatever hawks and hotheads might assert, a few home truths need to be directed at those who insist that a cataclysmic conflict between the US and China is imminent or inevitable.

These are in summary as follows.

There is zero chance of a clash between the two countries on, or remotely near, either's soil. There is not even a chance of something akin to the Cuban Missile Crisis. The idea is a fantasy.

The United States is, uniquely in our times, a global military force, with a presence dispersed across the planet. China is not. Its primary aim is to assert its supremacy in its own region, but even that is a tall order with Japan, South Korea, Taiwan, India and Australia (and others such as Indonesia, Vietnam and the Philippines) having every reason to resist its attempt to make the South China Sea its own waters. China may print its favoured 'nine lines' on its own maps but its neighbours will have nothing of it. Individually they might be weak compared with Beijing but collectively they have some muscle.

The American and Chinese militaries are thus nowhere close to approximately equal in their power. The US outspends

China by a massive amount and furthermore directs that money less towards personnel for the sake of numbers alone (as the People's Liberation Army has a tendency to do) but towards the military architecture and infrastructure which would wipe out any enemy in combat.

What is more, the Pentagon is set under a Republican President and Congress to reap additional revenues and rewards not only because the baseline budget will certainly be increased but as European (and other) allies are obliged by the Trump White House to spend considerably more on their own defence, which will allow money to be redirected towards the Asian theatre if wanted. The sizeable increase in Chinese military expenditure of the past fifteen years will be much more difficult to sustain as growth rates fall and the need to keep the public sated economically increases. Just as the assumption that there will be a crossover in GDP between the United States and China at any point soon has, correctly, been put on ice, the idea that there may be anything like a crossover in the military expenditure between the two is preposterous. The US will literally outgun all comers.

Which makes a war over Taiwan even more remote. That would be the case if China could summon up double the resources for its military overnight (which it cannot). The technical difficulties in any scheme for a surprise attack are impossible to swerve. Taiwan is now better positioned than ever to defend itself if a full-scale invasion were to be launched, especially as such a plan could not be hidden. China would have to assume that the United States would intervene if it attempted to snatch Taiwan and if it did then a host of others would be obliged to reinforce that effort. The costs on multiple levels would be astronomical. It is just about the one course of action that could endanger the CCP itself. It might yearn to bring

Taiwan back into the fold, but it does not have the capacity to compel it to. It has the might to ensure that Taiwan does not declare independence (unless there were to be a Republican President who actively urged the Democratic Progressive Party to take such a bold step), but it cannot stop Taiwan from being in every respect, bar a formal declaration, independent. Nor will the offer of 'one country, two systems' ever be trusted after the treatment seen in Hong Kong.

The 'hot war' assertion does not hold because of its abject impracticalities. The worst-case scenario is that of the 'tepid war' in which China habitually rattles the cage in and around Taiwan but is never capable of pushing further. The 'Cold War' model is not fit for purpose because even if the animosity level between the US and China intensifies, the conditions that were the contours of the international system with the US and USSR from the 1940s to the 1980s do not hold for 2026–2049.

The question that truly counts is a different one. It is whether in the political and hence the military sphere, the US and China will have to live with a cold peace of suspicion and subterfuge (with a negative effect for both and the wider world as well) or whether something considerably more enlightened might be available. Neither nation is an innate threat to the other. Taiwan is not what the divided city of Berlin was in the 1940s, 1950s and 1960s. Both countries could do with lower military expenditure (although it devotes less to it, China would benefit the most from shifting what it has back from guns to butter). The acid test for 2026 to 2049 is the leadership to achieve this.

There is one final factor to consider, although how to quantify its effect is not clear. Xi Jinping has become increasingly attached to purging the most senior ranks of the military whenever there is the slightest suspicion of corruption. His zeal for that has intensified of late. In early 2026, it emerged that General Zhang Youxia (who had previously been thought especially close to his leader and the last remaining figure in the high command with combat experience) had been accused of selling nuclear secrets to the Americans. Another very prominent soldier, General Liu Zhenli, also appeared to have fallen from favour. This meant that five of the six career officers appointed to the Central Military Commission in 2022 were no longer in place. All that remained were Xi himself and General Zhang Shengmin (his enforcer). At the Communist Party Central Committee level, at least twenty-nine of the forty-four military members selected in 2022 did not seem to be in place three years later. This cannot be an asset to the armed forces.

The focus on Taiwan and the military aspect of the US–China relationship is understandable. Yet it risks 'fighting the last war': an outlook based on the US–USSR rivalry of decades past. It is not likely to be an accurate or a helpful basis for analysing Washington and Beijing in the 2020s and 2030s.

10

HOW TO WIN FRIENDS AND INFLUENCE PEOPLE?

The battle for hearts and minds frequently involves an appeal to wallets. For a very long period, China, while more than content to court politically members of the Non-Aligned Movement that was established during the Cold War (often competing with India while doing so), had little interest in becoming directly involved as an investor in developing countries (beyond itself). This shifted very slightly under Jiang Zemin who promoted a 'Go Out' policy and encouraged a 'China Western Development' strategy. These were modest in ambition (and expense) and close to home. The notion of a much bigger vision with China active not just in Central Asia and East Asia, but the Middle East, Africa, Latin America and even to a degree Europe was never on the cards. Not only would the expense of it be excessive, it would have been at odds with the approach to international affairs that Deng Xiaoping had impressed upon his colleagues, namely that China should keep its head down, bide its time and never put itself forward to be a leader. In a world in which others may seek the spotlight, China should punch below its weight.

Almost immediately upon assuming the unchallenged leadership of the Communist Party, Xi Jinping reversed course. China would no longer keep its head down; the years of biding its time had run their course, it had to be prepared to assume a role in what Xi considered to be 'major-country diplomacy'. The centrepiece for this was to be the Belt and Road Initiative (BRI).

What is the Belt and Road Initiative?

Despite its central importance to China's engagement in international relations, the amount of money that has been spent on it (an estimated $1 trillion) and its astonishing ambition, the BRI is only faintly familiar and dimly understood by even sophisticated observers of global politics in the United States and Europe. It is the most focused attempt by a country to steer others in its economic and cultural direction since the US Marshall Plan after the Second World War (although the BRI is supposed to be driven by commercial logic, it is not an aid programme). It is absolutely at the heart of Beijing's foreign policy under Xi.

It has the official title of 'The Silk Road Economic Belt and 21st Century Maritime Silk Road Development Strategy'. Its stated objective is 'to construct a unified large market and make full use of both international and domestic markets, through cultural exchange and integration, to enhance mutual understanding and trust of member nations, resulting in an innovative pattern of capital flows, talent pools and technology databases'.

A detailed mission statement, the *Visions and Actions on Jointly Building Belt and Road*, was published in 2015. It was known more popularly within China as 'One Belt, One Road' until rebranded as the Belt and Road Initiative in 2016. It has been overseen since late 2014 by very high-level Chinese political figures, initially chaired by Zhang Gaoli (a Vice Premier of China and a member of the Standing Committee of the Politburo at the time). Among others who were responsible for its acceleration was Wang Huning, who later became (and remains) a member of the Standing Committee of the Politburo himself and who has been the ideologist-in-chief within the highest echelons of the CCP for about thirty years. He is not in any sense an economist or an engineer. He exists to shape Party philosophy. This would suggest that the BRI is rather more than a conventional if large development effort but has a political edge as well. By happy coincidence, the whole BRI is due to be finished in 2049, the one-hundredth anniversary of the proclamation of the People's Republic of China and the CCP acquiring power.

There are two main components of the BRI, and they were announced separately in late 2013.

The first was then described as 'The Silk Road Economic Belt' in a speech made by Xi Jinping at Nazarbayev University in Astana, Kazakhstan in September 2013 on an official visit to that country. It would be a 'Belt' that would allow for a new overland route or routes for road and rail transportation through a series of mostly landlocked Central Asian countries. It has the deliberate echo of the original Silk Road which was established during the Han dynasty (206 BCE–220 CE) when it broke out of eastern China and started to look and push westwards. It traversed what today are Afghanistan, Kazakhstan, Kyrgyzstan, Tajikistan, Turkmenistan and Uzbekistan as well as touching upon contemporary India and Pakistan. It enabled trade to flourish and ultimately allowed Chinese commerce a (long and complex) means to European markets.

The second was dubbed 'The 21st Century Maritime Silk Road' when it was launched in October 2013 by Xi Jinping in an address to the Indonesian Parliament while in that country for an ASEAN summit in October 2013. The notion of a maritime road is an innately strange formula. It did not really have a historical precedent and was more sweeping in scope than the 'Belt'. The 'Road' would connect a set of sea routes through South-East Asia to South Asia to the Middle East to Africa (and, as it turned out, via the Suez Canal the 'Road' reached Europe). In a number of cases this would involve the restoration of old ports or the creation of new ones.

A third aspect of the initiative would emerge later. This was the 'Digital Silk Road', a new component of the BRI that first surfaced in 2015. It included the offer of digital technological development, the development of digital standards and the expansion of digital infrastructure. It also opened the door to Chinese digital technology as an alternative to that of the United States.

An additional if rather boutique offshoot was educational. In addition to physical investment, China would also offer a large number of academic scholarships to those willing to attend universities in that country in preparation for involvement with the BRI thereafter. This chimed with a broader effort by the Party to make China an importer as well as exporter of students.

How has the BRI operated?

The Belt part of it involved six substantial urban land corridors:

- the China–Pakistan Economic Corridor;
- the New Eurasian Land Bridge including the Silk Road Railway;

- the China–Mongolia–Russia Economic Corridor;
- the China–Central Asia–West Asia Corridor (extending all the way to Turkey);
- a China–Indochina Peninsula Economic Corridor (which ends at Singapore);
- a Trans-Himalayan Multi-Dimensional Connectivity Network.

The Road part mostly follows but then moves beyond sea lanes that were already being used by more than half of the world's container ships (although many of them involved lengthy and not very efficient routes, not least because of antiquated port facilities). The blueprint was to link Hanoi, Kuala Lumpur, Singapore and Jakarta, then Colombo, Malé in the Maldives, on to Mombasa, Kenya, then over to Djibouti (where China was in the process of obtaining its own base) up through the Red Sea, taking in Haifa, Istanbul and Athens before ending at Trieste which in turn would allow access by railway for freight to be moved into Central and Eastern Europe.

The 'Digital Silk Road' meant that China would build thirty-four terrestrial cables and dozens of underwater cables within twelve BRI affiliates in Asia, Africa and Europe from 2017 to 2022. Alibaba and Huawei between them provided many of the components and 5G networks.

This was clearly a comprehensive effort to create something entirely novel. It had the potential to enhance trade flows in more than 150 countries, cut the cost of global trade (sharply in some circumstances) and provide a direct economic stimulus to the GDP of a collection of countries predominantly but not exclusively in Central Asia, East Asia and the Pacific Rim. Almost every study by an international organisation attested to its worth. So did independent institutions. The Centre for

Economic and Business Research, as an illustration, asserted that it would increase overall world GDP by more than $7 trillion by the year 2040.

How did the funding work?

There were a variety of means by which the financing functioned. The scope of the BRI was huge. It would involve classic infrastructure investment in buildings, roads, railways, power grids, and allied requirements such as iron and steel capacity if it was not there already. None of this would be cheap and an assessment of the costs and benefits of the project would be haphazard.

There were occasions where China simply built and paid for facilities on the assumption that it would never see a financial return on them. Beijing put billions into Afghanistan, Bangladesh, Nepal, Pakistan and Sri Lanka, all of which had been politically sympathetic in the past and were likely to be even more reliable associates in the future thanks to the investment.

This was, however, where the minority of the money went. Most of it came in the form of loans that were backed by collateral such as the right to a mine, land or a port in the event that the debt could not be serviced. Somewhat controversially, if the arrangement involved port facilities then the operator would usually be China Merchants Port, a Hong Kong conglomerate that on paper had no connection whatsoever with the rulers of Beijing, but few accepted that thesis.

The appeal to borrowers was that there were often no other sources of supply available (neither the US nor European nor transnational lenders such as the World Bank would touch the country or the leadership concerned); if there was any potential competition then the terms being set out by China were ordinarily less demanding (although far from easy) and the projects when they received the green light would proceed quickly without delays resulting from considerations of human rights, the environmental aspects of the schemes, working conditions, the quality of project management at the host end, or risk of corruption. Put like that, they were a one-way bet as far as many in Africa, and poorer Latin American states especially, could see their interests.

The consequence was that China suddenly found that it was the largest bilateral lender in the world, a standing that affords a certain prestige and power but weighs upon a balance sheet.

The cost could not be met by the taxpayers of China exclusively. Beijing did initiate a Silk Road Fund of its own but leant on others over which it had sway to be supporters of the initiative. These included the China Investment Corporation, the China Development Bank, the Export-Import Bank of China, the Bank of China (which lent $185 billion between 2015 and 2020) and the Industrial and Commercial Bank of China (which had lent in excess of $100 billion by 2019).

There was a critical additional actor whose existence became intimately entwined with the BRI.

The Asian Infrastructure Investment Bank was first mooted by China in 2013 at around the same time as the first two strands of the BRI (the 'Belt' and the 'Road') were initially floated. It came into being at the very end of 2015 despite the United States being deeply suspicious about it.

In rapid order, the AIIB shot to become the second-largest multilateral development institution after the long-established World Bank (over which the Americans had huge influence). It had signed up 110 members. Of these forty-two were in

Asia, twenty-six in Europe (including the UK which in a rare move decided to engage despite disapproving noises from the Obama administration), twenty-two in Africa, ten in Oceania, eight in South America and two in North America. It would be based in Beijing but have a stellar international cast list among its most senior ranks (the Liberal Democrat ex-Chief Secretary to the Treasury Danny Alexander was the best-known UK representative). It was independent of the Chinese government but unlikely to act against its wishes. It would be a crucial backer of the BRI with $160 billion invested into its various projects (almost always at the most commercially robust end of the spectrum but that freed China itself up to lend elsewhere).

Needless to state, this was a very large sum of money being deployed in a fast and furious way.

Who are now involved with the BRI?

If affiliation alone is deemed the measure of success, then the BRI has managed that in spades. By 2024, barely a decade after it was put forward as an idea, almost 150 countries were formally involved with the BRI and between them they constituted about 75 per cent of the global population and 50 per cent of global GDP. Xi Jinping would doubtless consider this to be a very personal triumph.

As of 2025 there are 148 nations plus China itself that are participants in the BRI (and three nations that were in, but have withdrawn: Estonia, Italy and the Philippines). Panama, after intense pressure from the Trump administration through Secretary of State Marco Rubio, has announced that it too will not renew its membership when it expires. Many of the participants are predictable, as well as geographically logical. Others spark more curiosity.

There are three sub-categories of members that raise eyebrows (notably in Washington).

The first is that there are no less than sixteen members of the European Union involved and four other states (Moldova, Montenegro, North Macedonia and Serbia) that are seeking to join the EU in the not-too-distant future (whether they will be accepted is debateable). The largest players, France, Germany, Italy and Spain, were either never in or, in Italy's case, in then smartly out, but Poland is an active member and has pursued its own economic alliance with China. It would come as a surprise to some that the likes of Austria, Portugal and even Luxembourg have been recruited. Belgium and the Netherlands have not followed Luxembourg in. Almost all of the central European states (Hungary, the Czech Republic, Slovakia, Slovenia and Croatia) have signed up. Across the Baltic states, Latvia and Lithuania are in, but Estonia now sits outside it. None of the Scandinavian nations (or Finland) have decided that the Belt runs up to them.

The second is that the Road element has extended right across the Atlantic and includes nations on the very eastern Pacific coast as well. There are almost twenty Latin American and Caribbean countries that have been content to take Chinese money, predominantly so that they can upgrade their port facilities. This has allowed China to become an economic partner in a theatre in which the United States has, from the Monroe Doctrine onwards, insisted that other powers would not be welcome to acquire leverage in what it deems to be its backyard. As noted, that China, albeit via China Merchants Port, was allegedly effectively in charge of the Panama Canal, which the United States had built, paid for and run until it agreed to hand it over to the Panamanians, brought a fierce denunciation from Donald Trump in his Inauguration Address and an unsubtle threat to seize the facility again if Panama did not evict its Chinese guests.

The third set of shocks is the nations of the Persian Gulf, many of them massively rich as a result of oil and distinctly dependent on the United States for their security. Yet that has not stopped Bahrain, Kuwait, Oman, Qatar, Saudi Arabia and the United Arab Emirates from aligning themselves with an enterprise that has always had 'Made in China' stamped all over it.

Then there is the intrigue in those who have not chosen to be associated with this initiative. Italy was the only G7 nation ever to have been within the fold but Prime Minister Giorgia Meloni, perhaps with American opinion firmly in her mind, decided that it did not add sufficient value. Australia was offered a role but eventually turned it down (annoying China as it did) but New Zealand, which often moves in lockstep with its much bigger brother, went in, following a pattern of Wellington seeing Beijing differently to Canberra. The first free trade deal that China ever did with a developed economy was with New Zealand. India not only rebuffed the invitation but dislikes the support that has been lavished on the road network of Pakistan, which could easily (and deliberately) end up serving Pakistan's military in the event of war. It has openly sought to throw rocks at the scheme (but with no reward as far as Bangladesh and Sri Lanka are concerned). Japan and South Korea are out as well (Taiwan did not receive an invitation). Argentina thought about going in but presumably under President Javier Milei has dropped the idea. Chile, like its poorer neighbours Bolivia and Peru, is a BRI member (which appears odd). Brazil declined to take part in October 2024 which was unexpected, considering its role within the BRICS alliance.

All told, nevertheless, acquiring almost 150 members when what is on offer is mostly loans is a political accomplishment of some order. The BRI has almost certainly reached the zenith of its membership as almost everyone who might have a reason to consider it has had the chance to do so. In any case, as will be outlined shortly, the pipeline of loans was curtailed for practical considerations during the pandemic and then did not come back at anything like the old scale.

That does not mean that Xi Jinping has any intention of winding the BRI down in the near future. As far as he is concerned, it has been invaluable on several fronts, not least his desire for China to be viewed as a leader in the world and for his concept of a global order to have an audience.

What does China get out of the BRI?

This should not be seen as some sort of ego trip for one Chinese leader. There are a number of advantages to the BRI that serve domestic as well as foreign policy purposes.

It is a de facto form of regional policy within China, in that it hardens connections between the wealthy and densely populated south and east of the country and the vast but sparse west, notably the enormous but troublesome province of Xinjiang (to which the authorities in Beijing would like to attract more Han Chinese to make it a more manageable place and suppress Uyghur sentiments), making western China the gateway to a huge route out all the way to Turkey and the Black Sea. There is a rational self-interest in aspiring to rebalance stark geographical inequalities inside China.

It is a means of absorbing what at times has become excessive manufacturing capacity.

It is a mechanism by which China's very high savings ratio (its consumers, despite official prompting, do not spend in the manner of their equivalents in Europe or North America) finds an outlet. This was particularly useful when the rush of foreign direct investment from overseas was crowding out domestic savings for deployment in the Chinese private sector (although this has dried up).

It has enabled Chinese companies to explore new markets, some of which in Africa and Latin America are unlikely to have materialised as opportunities if the BRI had not happened. This has been markedly so for those involved in the high technology space in China and for those championing China's versions of the internet in opposition to the American World Wide Web.

It has helped expand the use of the Chinese currency (the yuan/renminbi) while allowing it to remain under the control of the state in a way that is not acceptable for reserve currencies.

During the Covid-19 pandemic, it allowed Beijing (temporarily) to establish a 'health silk road', a means by which Chinese vaccines could be distributed at speed throughout the region (although it has to be said that those rather basic vaccines were far less effective than those created in the US and UK).

Then there are what might be labelled as the more strictly realpolitik arguments in its favour.

The loans do more than attract an interest repayment. They can create a form of political dependence among those who receive them, have to service them and (hopefully) repay them. The past decade has seen China able to mobilise something of a bloc vote among African and some Latin American nations on issues that Beijing determines are of real importance to it. It cannot be a coincidence that this political support is so uniform or that it is drawn so starkly from those who have a financial stake as debtors within the BRI. As temporary membership of the UN Security Council also rotates around the continents and regions of the world, the BRI enables China to have the option of calling in favours at the highest level of governance.

There is a special salience in China being capable of developing ports, overseeing them (if only through the nominally independent China Merchants Port) and, if the debts involved are not repaid, then extracting additional authority over them in return for not sending the bailiffs in. That it was the loss of control of their own ports during the One Hundred Years of Humiliation may be a further factor at work here.

Critics would, as a case study, direct attention towards Hambantota International Port, a desirable deep-water port in Sri Lanka, over which China Merchants Port now has a ninety-nine-year lease. The extent to which this acquisition is part of an explicit 'debt-trap' strategy is heatedly disputed but the accusation has been made, and time will tell if other similar ports end up the same way.

Even if the 'debt-trap' accusation is excessive, increased influence over ports around the globe makes a lot of sense from Beijing's perspective. They help to ease what have been pinch points such as the Straits of Hormuz and Malacca, which China relies upon for the free flow of oil, but which are always at the risk of closure or obstruction either due to military conflict or if the American Navy were to decide on the orders of the Oval Office to make life inconvenient.

There is also, to be more conspiratorial, the chance that ports being redesigned at the behest of China could be configured so that they had a dual use, not merely commercial but a welcome berth for Chinese vessels in the neighbourhood. The absence of a network of ports and single-use military bases in deep-water locations is a very substantial weakness for China compared with its American rival. Anything that even partially corrected this disequilibrium would be worth obtaining. And it has the asset that it would all be done by stealth rather than in an open signing ceremony between the parties.

This was probably not what attracted Xi Jinping to the BRI at the outset (although it may have become more appealing as the relationship between Beijing and Washington has deteriorated). In this instance, the simple explanation for why he has made this his cause remains convincing. He has cast off Deng's desire for China to concentrate almost entirely on its own economy and society and wants to be at the helm of a nation which punches at least at its weight if not above it, but certainly not below it as a matter of deliberate calculation. The BRI serves that purpose.

Past and future US responses to the BRI

It took some time for the United States to acknowledge the importance of the BRI, in part because it did not believe that anything like the scale of resources would be thrown at it as has plainly been the case. The proverbial penny did not really drop until there was a wider volte-face in Democratic and Republican elite circles alike on the bigger question of whether 'strategic engagement' with Beijing was still the right approach, or a fool's errand.

The response, such as it has been, has had an *ad hoc* quality. It was far too late to knock on the doors of those countries that had accepted Chinese loans and urge them to return the cash. Some sway could be exercised over countries which were involved in the arrangement in order to improve the efficiency of trade routes rather than because they wanted to join the queue at the Bank of Beijing (which may have triggered Italy's change of heart). But there has not been a stampede out of the BRI and the US cannot force one to occur.

Insofar as there has been a proactive response at all, it has shown that imitation is indeed the sincerest form of flattery. In 2018 Congress legislated for the BUILD Act, which President Trump then signed as an explicit reaction to the realisation that the BRI had obtained true traction. The law (BUILD stands for Better Utilization of Investments Leading to Development) knocked together different institutions within the existing apparatus in Washington to create a new Development Finance Corporation with a $60 billion budget, but it was to function within constraints that were unattractive to impoverished nations.

When the Biden administration came in, it sought to use the aftermath of the pandemic to reboot the American approach in this area. In 2021, on its own and through the G7, it came up with the Build Back Better World Initiative, which was supposed to mobilise investment. At about the same time, the European Union attempted to chip in with its Global Gateway, a $300 billion infrastructure investment programme. Neither of them made it far off the ground. The political will might have been there, but the instant availability of cash was not.

Bureaucratic inertia meant that the proposed organisations existed more in name than in nature. To add insult to injury, China was now winning eight times as many contracts within the World Bank for infrastructure investment issued in its name than the United States had managed to secure.

Official Washington could sense the writing on the wall and did not care for the message. The esteemed Council on Foreign Relations assembled a taskforce in 2020–2021 to investigate the BRI and make recommendations as to whether and how to counter it. It accused the BRI of a number of sins. These included undermining global macroeconomic security by the terms on offer, which could result in a fresh debt crisis (China's terms made it very hard for a debtor to look towards the 'Paris Club' of western lenders for restructuring); undercutting, marginalising or subverting the World Bank (a Washington DC-based entity); subsidising market entry for state-owned enterprises and non-market companies; locking countries into carbon-intensive energy (China was quite willing to provide loans for those looking to invest in coal mines); and subverting global standards by ignoring crass project management and transparent corruption.

Assembling the charge sheet was straightforward enough; coming up with something that could now be done to counter the BRI was much more awkward. There were recommendations made that were worthy in spirit (such as enhanced US diplomacy to promote alternatives to the BRI and a vigorous anti-corruption campaign) and slightly more concrete proposals such as an extra $100 billion for research and development spending, reforming the new Development Finance Corporation (which even its creators would concede had been designed on the hoof) and mobilising the US technology sector to lead the charge for its own version of the Digital Silk Road.

There was nothing here that either the White House or Congress would be captivated by. It all had the aura of too little, too late. The BRI was too firmly established for the United States to be able to disrupt it or set up an alternative which would divert existing members towards it. Everything amounted to trying to shut the door after the horse had bolted. If the returning Trump team had any cunning plan of its own, it was well disguised with the emphasis instead on gutting US aid.

Game over?

Is this then an example of a straight sets victory for Xi Jinping and China? On the surface it would seem as if Xi Jinping has played his cards rather well and held most of the aces in development. This could turn out to be the case, but there are also reasons to hold fire on that conclusion.

The first is that the BRI sprayed too much money around in too many places while engaging in the most rudimentary due diligence. The critical investment criterion at times seemed to be 'Will they take the money?' Even if Covid had not for practical reasons obliged the lights to be turned off and the punchbowl taken away, a reset would have been unavoidable.

The second is that China either directly or indirectly has a lot of dubious debtors. It has already had to forgive (comparatively small) interest-free loans to seventeen African countries. That is small fry compared with some of the money that will probably never come back to it. The outstanding loans associated with the BRI amount to 25 per cent of China's GDP, and this is a nation that at home already has a debt-to-GDP ratio of 300 per cent, even though it is the second-largest economy globally. What will be the impact on China and its fragile banking system if the debt cannot be repaid?

Finally, what will be the effect if it attempts to call in the assets that have served as collateral? What will be its standing then with the developing nations which it had assiduously befriended? What appeal will Xi's call for a cause of common destiny have in these conditions? Will China actually seize that to which it is contractually entitled? Or will the debt enter never-never land?

There is enough doubt as well as debt out there for BRI to stand for Brash, Risky and Inadvisable.

11

TECHNOLOGY – THE TRUE FRONTIER

Much has been made of a current and continuing US–China 'trade war'. Yet in many respects this is a misleading line of thinking. China remained – at least until the tariff turmoil of 2025 – the third-largest trading partner for the United States after Canada and Mexico. Although this is assumed to be something akin to one-way traffic (Chinese exports to the US), the revenues that American firms obtain in the other direction exceed those from Japan, Germany and the United Kingdom combined. This made the notion of separating out the two economies from each other entirely very difficult.

That is hardly surprising. Much of US–China economic engagement and trade is uncontentious in character. Many aspects of it might be caught up in the tariffs imposed during the initial Trump administration (2018–2019) and then the much more intense series of tariffs that he imposed almost from the moment that he resumed office in January 2025, but the products are still comparatively mundane. Soybeans, for example, are rarely thought of in terms of national security. When certain Republicans talk of 'de-coupling' the US and China on trade, this is not their target.

The true frontier

The same cannot be said for certain transformative technologies. Both the Belt and Road Initiative and the alleged risk of a Chinese invasion of Taiwan are, if the pun will be excused, red herrings. That they acquire attention is understandable. They are, in different but not wildly dissimilar ways, very visible. They involve assets and activities that are relatively straightforward for outsiders to comprehend.

This is not the case for what has become, and will probably remain, the real frontier. The struggle (to use a word that Xi Jinping is particularly fond of articulating) is over the presumed technologies of the future, a category of innovations that can be at least as much of an agent of economic change as steam, the railways, electrification, the internet or advanced mobile telephones have proved. Indeed, those close to the sectors concerned, including artificial intelligence, quantum computing and big data, insist that they will have an even more seismic impact on the economy and our society.

At the most dramatic, it is a vision best set out by a British futurologist, Jason Bradbury, who declared that the 2020s would be the 'thousand-year decade'. It would involve as fundamental a set of technological advances in the space of ten years as had been witnessed in the preceding thousand years. This was, it should be conceded, a pronouncement made before the Covid-19 pandemic interrupted ordinary existence.

Even so, if he were only 10 per cent right in his analysis and the 2020s proved to be the 'hundred-year decade' then that would be significant enough in itself. Even this appeared to be unlikely in the opening years of the 2020s until the sudden advance of artificial intelligence through OpenAI and its release of ChatGPT in 2023 threw open the doors publicly to a realm of research that had until that point been hidden. What seemed improbable looked rather more possible. The sense of there being an equivalent to the 'space race' of the 1960s between the United States and the USSR was now real, except that the reward to the winner would not be like the mere symbolism of being the first to land a man and plant a flag on the surface of the moon, but a much bigger economic prize. The working assumption on all sides was that first-mover advantage here would be really critical.

This has become the actual, meaningful theatre of contest if not conflict for the USA and China. A better military model than a 'war' would be 'special operations'. There is undoubtedly an intense special operations activity being mounted, and by both sides, and it is increasing at some pace. The primary field for this is semiconductors and the principal protagonist is the US acting against China.

The first salvo

On 7 October 2022, the Bureau of Industry and Security, a small and seemingly obscure office of the US Department of Commerce, acting upon recent legislative authority, issued a 139-page document entitled 'Commerce Implements New Export Controls on Advanced Computing and Semiconductor Manufacturing Items to the People's Republic of China (PRC)'. It might not be the snappiest of names, but the strategy behind it can be rendered far more succinct. It was an overt attempt to cripple China's capacity to acquire and from there develop top-quality semiconductors.

As a consequence, 721 Chinese companies, organisations and people were placed on what was then described as an 'entity list' that eliminates or restricts their ability to buy these products from the US. That number was certain to increase further (it did) as Washington devoted more resources to this.

Why semiconductors?

Semiconductors are a staple of much of the core technology that the contemporary world relies on. They need to be very small to be of maximum efficiency. The primary semiconductor in a state-of-the-art smartphone has between ten and twenty billion transistors. But these are considered rather basic by the standards of the sector and inexpensive. They are, to borrow the British phrase, 'cheap as chips'. Even in this comparatively straightforward sphere, however, China has long struggled (as will be set out) to secure a convincing domestic supply chain. At times in the 2020s, Beijing spent more on bulk importing run-of-the-mill semiconductors than it did on importing oil.

The real contest, however, is over the semiconductors of the future. They need to become smaller and contain even more information, and the scientific and technological race to achieve this is in its early stages. The next generation of semiconductors is the spine of what artificial intelligence, among other developments, can deliver for the economy. Without them, all progress will be limited. This explains why semiconductors are the special operations in the US-Sino economic competition.

The great fall

China has sought to become a serious player in semiconductors for a very long time. State initiatives in this area date back to 1981. Despite four decades of industrial policy, the returns have been poor. China accounted for comfortably less than 10 per cent of overall global production in 2020, and a sizeable proportion of that figure involved the lower-to-mid-end in terms of semiconductor capabilities. For the most significant element in the market – what might be called super semiconductors – China is a largely inconsequential country. Indeed, it has been well short of a presence in the top quartile in terms of quality. To make matters worse, one massive company located off its shores in the South China Sea, Taiwan Semiconductor Manufacturing Company (TSMC), is superior to any found within China.

This has long been a cause of irritation and can have some surreal side-effects as periodic attempts are made to ignite the domestic market for semiconductor production through lavish subsidies. In early 2020, by coincidence as Covid-19 was publicly emerging, a particularly prominent and fiscally promiscuous programme of incentives was publicised. In the following ten months, almost sixty thousand new semiconductor-related companies were established in China. That might appear to be a policy success, except that the majority (probably the vast majority) were set up in the middle of nowhere, with no transformative technology to exploit, nor any serious blueprint for innovation. It was an invitation for opportunists to seek to cash in what was virtually a blank cheque from the state.

Why is acquiring super semiconductors so hard for China?

There are compelling reasons why this abject failure has occurred.

The first is that developing the core infrastructure for super semiconductors is so eye-wateringly expensive. Semiconductor factories, or 'fabs' as they are known, are easily the most expensive form of factories in the world, and not only that cost but the sheer complexity is a massive barrier to entry.

This has become more true as the technology itself evolves. The paradox is that as the operating costs of producing ever more sophisticated semiconductors come down, the capital expenditure required to engage in that production reaches prohibitively high levels. It is a vast bar to clear.

The additional resources required were neatly captured by *The Economist* in September 2024. It observed:

> a dynamic of the semiconductor industry: as transistors, the main type of electronic component found in chips, have become smaller, the tools and factories to make them have become bigger and pricier. Brian Potter, of the Institute for Progress, an American think-tank, estimates that in the late 1960s a semiconductor fabrication plant (or fab) cost about $31 million in today's money. The newest fabs that TSMC, a Taiwanese giant, is building in Arizona will cost $20 billion each.

The second is that the equipment needed to compete at the highest level in semiconductors is not the sort that one can acquire off the shelf or build oneself on the basis of the right manual. To take one example, an Extreme Ultraviolet (EUV) lithography machine made by ASML, the sizeable Dutch conglomerate, can create structures as small as ten nanometres wide (unimaginably tiny) and is vital to the most pioneering forms of artificial intelligence. It does this through a laser, made by one and only one company (German as it happens), that can manipulate plasma to order by charging it to a heat that is forty times the surface temperature of the Sun. This laser has 457,329 parts to it. The entire EUV machine has more than 100,000 components overall, many of serious scarcity value.

The third aspect is the people. Even if an aspiring super semiconductor developer could divine how to construct the facilities needed (unlikely) and where to acquire the key technology (implausible), they would need a large number of extremely well-trained individuals to then work inside the fab. To state that the supply of such exceptionally qualified people is finite is a vast understatement.

What makes matters more challenging still for China is that all the theoretical suppliers of key assets are either based in the United States itself, or among its close allies in Asia (Japan, South Korea and Taiwan) or in Europe (Germany, the Netherlands and to a lesser extent the UK) or, in a niche context, the state of Israel. If the US wants to shut out China, then it has the means.

The US drive to cut China out of super semiconductors

Over the past five years or so, the US has had not only the means but the motivation to do this. In about 2018 (arguably a few years late), Washington realised that China's economic ambitions had changed. Beijing no longer aspired to engage in a dash to become the world's largest economy by GDP through high-volume, low-value manufacturing on a mass scale, but wanted to up-skill and to do so quickly. A situation in which it could only produce elementary semiconductors at home and had to rely on imports which fell short of the gold standard was not satisfactory.

The first Chinese company to seek to move into this virgin territory was Huawei, which was cheered on by, but took care to maintain a distance from, the Chinese government. Washington was alarmed by the prospect of many American companies and institutions becoming dependent on its (relatively cheap if not quite Super Bowl-level) technology. It was viewed as a high-tech Trojan Horse within the Trump administration. Citing national security concerns, from May 2019 Washington sought to take on and to take out Huawei through a series of targeted measures. The full force was felt later when the US issued what was a de facto blanket ban on US institutions doing business with Huawei. The company was fundamentally undermined and forced to retreat in order to enable it to survive. It did endure, despite the efforts of the US authorities, and speculation that a later smartphone, the Mate 60 Pro, has a chip that may allow for a 5G form of capacity suggests a make-shift effort has produced results.

The next move, from May 2020, involved the aggressive use of an existing Foreign Direct Product Rule to limit China's access to super semiconductor supplies. The new interpretation meant that not only could US-based companies not supply such items, but foreign firms which made items that are produced through US technology or software faced similar restrictions in this field. It was an extraordinary act of extra-territoriality as a matter of law but also a highly potent weapon to deploy.

In tandem with this came a vigorous campaign of onshoring super semiconductor assets to the US. The country had been responsible for 37 per cent of international semiconductor manufacturing in the 1990s but this had slipped back drastically to a disturbingly low 12 per cent by the 2020s. TSMC was the first target, being somewhere between courted and compelled to establish a new fab in Arizona. A deal was brokered in May 2020 to allow that $12 billion facility to break ground. This would be reinforced by an accord with Samsung to build a $17 billion fab in Texas (announced in November 2021) and then Intel agreeing to pursue a $20 billion fab in Ohio (January 2022). In the same year Wolfspeed (a US company) stated that it would establish a plant in North Carolina, Micron Technology promised a $20 billion presence in upstate New York and TSMC declared that it was committed to a second fab in Arizona (although the opening of the first facility was delayed).

As alluded to, while they might have very different policy preferences in many spheres, in this instance the end of what would prove to be the first Trump administration and the beginning of what turned out to be the sole Biden administration saw not merely a continuity in policy but an intensification of it. The Biden people built on the base that the Trump team had left behind. It could be read as nothing less than a Trump–Biden declaration of intent aimed right at China. When he returned to Washington, Mr Trump made the restoration of US self-sufficiency in this sector an absolute priority. Taiwan was permitted a comparatively low tariff rate (15 per cent) entirely contingent on the extent to which TSMC invested in the United States and, in a highly unorthodox move for a Republican President, the federal government took a 10 per cent stake in the troubled US chip manufacturer Intel. This amounted to a selective industrial policy.

The CHIPS and Science Act 2022

It would be compounded on the statute book. There were sections of the Inflation Reduction Act of 2022 which manifestly intended to strengthen the US against China in a number of sectors (such as the production of electric vehicles and the batteries that are central to them). The more forensic legislation came in the form of the CHIPS and Science Act (with CHIPS standing for Creating Helpful Incentives to Produce Semiconductors) which also became law in August 2022.

The essence of the Act is that it provides almost $280 billion in new funding to support domestic research and manufacturing of semiconductors in general (but the best of them in particular) in the United States. This includes $39 billion in outright subsidies for chip manufacturing on US soil and an additional 25 per cent investment tax credit for the costs of manufacturing equipment and $15 billion for semiconductor research and workforce training. The open objective is to counter and contain China.

The final text bolted together a number of alternative proposals embraced in the House and Senate. Division A is the CHIPS Act of 2022. Division B is the Research and Development, Competition and Innovation Act. In a bizarre twist there is also a Division C which comprises the Supreme Court Security Funding Act of 2022 and is utterly unrelated to semiconductors. All of which serves to show that, no matter how clever ChatGPT might turn out to be, it will never be able to comprehend the American Congress.

This was formidable public backing for the super semiconductor sector. It was also, by modern US political standards, an uncontentious measure (despite the price tag). Virtually every Democrat in the House of Representatives and the Senate voted for it (the notionally independent Senator Bernie Sanders of Vermont voted against it). They were joined by seventeen Republicans in the Senate including the Minority Leader. Even in the hyper-partisan House, twenty-four Republicans endorsed the proposal. Those who did not assent were not actually against the law as such but disliked the shameless hand-out to sections of Silicon Valley that it involved, a leading constituency when it comes to fundraising for the Democratic Party, not only in California but nationally. The Republican Governors in Texas and Ohio, which stood to see shiny new fabs arrive first, were entirely content to salute the CHIPS approach. The US has thus devised a comprehensive battle plan for the super semiconductor contest to come. It has done so by as close to a consensus as is practical in what is such a polarised political period.

Aligning American allies

The United States had created a legislative Great Wall to ensure that it, rather than China, would be the beneficiary of any Great Leap Forward that might occur in transformational technologies. This involved some risks. A fundamental change in technology, involving a wholly novel type of super semiconductor or even something else entirely unexpected, could render the entire approach redundant. There have been plenty of examples where those who have invested in what seemed to be the certainties of the future have found themselves overtaken by events. Even if the bet had been made in the right place, shutting China out of super semiconductors might make it even more determined to throw everything at creating an independent capacity of its own and in some secrecy. Fear of a 'sputnik moment', akin to the sudden launch of a Soviet space satellite, remained serious.

It was unlikely, though, that such a shock could occur at any speed unless China could find supplies that would enable it to launch cutting-edge technologies of its own. This was plainly not going to be with the assistance of the United States. There were other countries that could be useful.

However, the US was determined that no such assistance would be forthcoming. It went to remarkable lengths to impose its will on its allies. The primary actor here was Jake Sullivan, the National Security Advisor to President Biden, based within the White House itself. Mr Sullivan was, in one sense, an unexpected Sinophobe. He had spent many years as a fully signed-up member of the mainstream Washington position that strategic engagement with China would ultimately trigger a degree of political and social liberalisation in that country and thus serve the cause of peace and prosperity. He was probably still in that camp as late as November 2016 when a senior advisor to the Clinton team (and indeed was widely regarded as her National Security Advisor in waiting). By the time that he took up that position under Mr Biden, his views on the US–China relationship in general and the question of Chinese access to key technologies had altered dramatically. The dove had become a hawk.

Just how much so was illustrated by a stunning interview published in the January/February 2025 issue of *Wired*, the leading US technology magazine. It is unclear when the dialogue (entitled 'The New Cold Warrior' by Issie Lapowsky) took place, as there is no reference to the result of the election in November 2024, so it could have been conducted before the return of Donald Trump to the Oval Office had been confirmed. If so, it is all the more striking as, had Kamala Harris been elected, Mr Sullivan would almost certainly have been on her shortlist to serve as the next Secretary of State.

Two elements of what Mr Sullivan revealed speak volumes about US policy in this sector.

The first is a personal reassessment of policy, which Democrats as well as Republicans have taken:

> If technology is being used more for ill than good, if the rules of the road are being set by our authoritarian competitors, if the technologies of the future are invented elsewhere and not here, that's going to mean less security, less jobs, and less productivity in the United States. I don't want to see that world.

The second is the extent to which Mr Sullivan was content to let it be known he was corralling allies. The article recounts at length a meeting between Mr Sullivan and his equivalents from Japan and the Netherlands, at which it was ensured that those two countries will march in lockstep with the US in its attempt to contain China in the super semiconductor theatre. Although hardly diplomatic reading in Tokyo or The Hague, where elites would have favoured privacy, a sense of priority here is manifest:

> Over the course of several hours, sitting inside a meeting room at Blair House … the three men ironed out the precise contours of each country's controls, finalizing what would be included and how long they would have to act. By the time they left, they had a firm understanding in place.

If the United States does not shut China out of super semiconductors it will not be for lack of effort.

A pyrrhic victory?

The United States thus appeared to have a comprehensive blueprint for containing China. It was an obvious source of annoyance to Beijing. In a telephone call with President Biden in 2024, Xi Jinping protested against the policy and insisted that if the US continued attempting to block his country's technological development, then he would not 'sit back and watch'. What he could actually do about the situation, nevertheless, appeared very limited in nature.

However, in early 2025, two developments made it appear that China still had cards up its sleeve.

The first and the biggest shock arrived courtesy of the Hangzhou DeepSeek Artificial Intelligence Basic Research Technology Research Co., Ltd, or DeepSeek for short. This was a new Chinese AI company (it had been founded only in July 2023) based in Hangzhou, Zhejiang (a province that Xi Jinping had long ago led but was certainly not a technology centre in his time). It had been established to develop large language models (LLMs) of the form that ChatGPT represented.

The company was backed by a Chinese hedge fund known as High-Flyer, which had itself been co-founded by Liang Wenfeng, who had been trained as an engineer but moved into algorithms with an application to financial markets. He had clearly had some success as the fund was flush with cash. LLMs were a private passion at first rather than an outright business notion. He became CEO of DeepSeek, alongside the same position that he held at High-Flyer. He had been planning his pivot for some time as it emerged that he had managed to obtain 10,000 Nvidia A100 graphics processing units in 2021 before US restrictions on such sales of semiconductors were legally entrenched. While superior to anything that he could have acquired domestically, they were not of the very top flight. It would transpire that they were more than adequate for the objective that he now had in mind.

DeepSeek moved at high speed and in an unconventional fashion. It recruited intensely from new university graduates, and not just those with experience in this area. Alongside those with the most obvious degrees to work in artificial intelligence, Liang sought out others from a variety of academic disciplines to broaden what his model might be able to accomplish. DeepSeek swiftly released a series of products, but mostly of a highly technical kind which, except for a very few specialists, did not receive enormous attention even within China, never mind the United States. At this stage, the company appeared to be rather interesting but not exceptional. It flew largely below the radar even for those who lived and breathed the terrain of artificial intelligence.

All that ended on 20 January 2025, when DeepSeek launched the DeepSeek Chatbot – based on its DeepSeek-R1 model – and made it available for free via iOS and Android. The effect of this was little short of sensational. That, by accident or design, the launch date coincided with Inauguration Day in the United States served to magnify the impact. While arguably inferior to ChatGPT it appeared to perform at a very similar level to a model that was thought would take years to be emulated. What was utterly unexpected was the claim that it had been trained at a cost of less than $6 million, compared with the $100 million or more that it had taken to develop OpenAI's GPT-4 in 2023, while employing about one-tenth of Meta's comparable model Llama 3.1. It was also a massive hit with (American) consumers. Within a week it had surpassed ChatGPT as the most downloaded app on the iOS store in the United States. The market, it seemed, was immensely impressed.

The ripple effects of all this were seminal. Donald Trump, hardly an expert in this arena, publicly conceded that it was a 'wake-up call' to the American technology sector. Those at the helm of Nvidia, which had become one of the 'Magnificent Seven' US technology companies on the basis that it held the market for chips in artificial intelligence in its captivity, did not need to be woken up. They suffered an instant 18 per cent slump in their share value, knocking some $600 billion off their valuation (although this was swiftly more than recovered). Furthermore, DeepSeek was refining its product in closer to weeks rather than months or years. In March 2025, it released DeepSeek V3-0324 which improved the offer (still free) even further. An enormous investment by the likes of Microsoft, Google and Meta looked as if it may be vulnerable.

That sense of a reversal of fortune was compounded, among those who fully understood the domain, by another event in March 2025. This was the launch, again out of nowhere, of Manus-AI, the brainchild of another Chinese start-up company called Monica.im. This was a business that had been founded by Xiao Hong, a serial entrepreneur, with Yichao 'Peak' Ji as a fellow co-founder and the chief scientist. Even less was known about this business than had been divined about DeepSeek.

What caused such intense excitement was that Manus-AI seemed to be the first example of an autonomous artificial intelligence agent, one that could master extremely complicated tasks of its own accord and without direct and continuous human instructions. This was a technology in its infancy and as such it could be somewhat clunky, but a Rubicon of a sort had been crossed. If it could be perfected it would involve a completely new form of artificial intelligence with immense implications for humanity. It was some distance from anything akin to conventional commercialisation, but a genie of unknown kind had come out of a technological bottle. That it was Chinese sent alarm bells ringing in Silicon Valley, but also in

Washington DC where a crusade to contain China now resembled a pyrrhic policy victory.

Conclusion

It is far too soon to tell whether the CHIPS and Science Act of 2022 has been a waste of words or if the activities of Jake Sullivan as National Security Advisor will prove to be a misuse of his time. The fate of Manus-AI, as an experimental technology, is open to serious debate. It might, paradoxically, provide the clues that American competitors need to produce a better version. The bigger cause for concern, in the short term, will be DeepSeek, which has an immediate utility.

Yet the DeepSeek story is a complicated one, which may not have punctured the American strategy.

DeepSeek is a fascinating example of improvisation as much as innovation. It relies on the purchase of American semiconductors which were not, even back in 2021, the most sophisticated that Nvidia had to offer and whose updated equivalents would be extremely hard for DeepSeek or any other Chinese institution to obtain today. Much of what DeepSeek has done has been about the skilful application of open-source material, but at the pace of a sprint, rather than a marathon. The old dictum that in China the letters R&D stand for 'replicate and duplicate' still has some legitimacy. What the episode does show is that China can work around some of the obstacles that the Trump, then the Biden, and now the Trump II administrations will hurl at it. If it is always only playing catch-up, however, the Americans will remain ahead in the contest.

Furthermore, it is not 'China' as in the authorities in Beijing who were responsible for this coup. It emerged from the private sector, towards which it maintains an ambivalent relationship. The month after DeepSeek had been launched, Xi Jinping hosted a conference of entrepreneurs (with Jack Ma restored to a front row seat) and warmly shook Liang Wenfeng by the hand as if a national hero. The media outlets in the country most closely associated with the Party leadership, such as the *Global Times*, have been entirely content to cast DeepSeek as a national accomplishment.

Yet Liang has made the money out of which DeepSeek was created as a hedge fund CEO, engaged in what in other circumstances the Chinese President would dismiss as part of the 'fictitious economy' of financial speculation and not the 'real economy' that official China wishes to stimulate. He has an 84 per cent stake through two shell companies. He has managed to avoid certain provisions of China's AI regulations aimed at consumer-facing industries by insisting that DeepSeek is a research entity. If his triumph came out of the blue to the American government, that of China was equally blindsided. Will Xi Jinping be ready to allow the private sector to stay in the lead here? Will DeepSeek by one means or another fall within his orbit? Will it be anything like as effective with the state involved? The questions raised by its arrival are as taxing for those in Beijing as they are for Washington DC.

This was further demonstrated by Manus-AI. Far from being a vassal of the Chinese state, it had by early 2026 relocated to Singapore and then agreed to be acquired by Meta. This was not what Beijing wanted. Its regulators hit back.

It is often said that the United States and China are in an AI 'race'. If so, then they are competing in separate events. The US authorities are determined that American companies will be the first to achieve AI 'superintelligence' and then maintain that advantage as the technology advances further. China, on the other hand, strongly influenced by its forthcoming demographic challenge, appears to be more interested in 'super application', the widest possible adoption within its economy of AI, even if it is of the fast and cheap form, not the most superior. So, this may prove to be a 'race' in which it is possible for there to be two winners.

12

CHINA, 2026–2049

To attempt to think about China and the United States in almost a quarter of a century is an exercise that is at best extremely ambitious and at worst intellectually insane. No blueprint of any precision can possibly be offered. It should not even really be attempted. What may prove to be the most important development of them all – technological change of a truly transformational character – is by far the hardest to anticipate.

It is, nonetheless, possible and productive to engage in a more limited series of predictions. These are rooted in what Donald Rumsfeld, in a fabled Pentagon briefing of 12 February 2002, labelled as 'known knowns', rather than 'known unknowns' or 'unknown unknowns'. The definition of 'known knowns' here has to be stretched somewhat to include suppositions that strictly speaking are not 'known' in the absolute sense of that term, but that are exceptionally reasonable to assume, based on what has been observed in the past and present, will continue into the future. These factors should, logically, have a fundamental influence on how China and the United States separately and collectively evolve over the second quarter of the twenty-first century and how they come to regard each other.

For these purposes, five metrics will be considered for each country in turn. They are the likely political structure of the nation, the party system, the principal societal challenges, the nature of the economy and the foreign policy and national security outlook its leaders will be shaped by. What will be seen is that in certain spheres a high level of continuity can be expected. In other sectors, what is striking is how different China and the United States may be.

Political structure

Neither internal convulsion nor external shock is likely to change the fundamental nature of the political structure of China. Its main features are the Communist Party itself, the state insofar as it operates differently from the Party (which formally it does but in functional terms it often does not) and what is often an underappreciated feature of China's political structure: the fact that it combines what seems to be a highly centralised political system with a deeply decentralised governmental one.

The history of the Constitution of the People's Republic of China is, compared with that of the United States, short. There was a temporary constitutional order in place from 1949 to 1954 as, understandably, the first task for the Communist Party then was to secure authority and power, rather than mandate a commission to come up with a new constitution. The first Constitution was endorsed in 1954. There were major revisions to it in 1975 (with the influence of the Cultural Revolution still visible) and 1978 (but before Deng was unambiguously installed as Paramount Leader). The most recent version emerged in 1982, and while there have been amendments of some scale (arguably five that merit the term substantial), it has stood the test of time since then. Recent leaders have preferred to amend it to suit their own agendas (such as the inclusion of Xi Jinping Thought in 2017) rather than seek to rewrite the document wholesale and disturb the existing balance between the Party and society, the Party and the state, and the central and local administration of China.

The leading role of the Chinese Communist Party in national life is the fundamental dictum in this political structure. How the Party organises itself is crucial to how China operates. The supreme institution is the National Congress. This meets as a body once every five years and is a massive event in its scale and as a political moment. As it is a very large entity (in 2022 there were 2,296 voting delegates), there are constraints in what it can achieve in a fortnight of official deliberations. Despite these limitations, the discussions are meaningful. They are an opportunity to test the temperature of Party sentiment. Public dissent is unthinkable, private disagreement entirely normal.

On a more regular basis, the National Congress delegates its authority to a Central Committee. This consists, at the last count, of 205 full members and 171 alternate members. This is the starting point for a serious career in national politics. The Central Committee then elects the Politburo (at present twenty-four persons, all men at the moment, somewhat atypically) and from there the Politburo Standing Committee is not so much elected in the pure sense but emerges out of straw polls, consultations with senior figures including past members of the leadership, and a sense of the acceptable combination of ages, backgrounds and geographical biographies. It is emphatically not simply the hand-picked allies of the leader of the day, no matter how strong.

The Central Committee is also responsible for the selection of other key bodies. These include the secretariat to the Party itself (of which the General Secretary and his de facto chief of staff are the crucial players), the Central Military Commission of the Communist Party of China (chaired by the Paramount Leader but otherwise dominated by very senior military figures) and the Central Commission for Discipline Inspection, the entity responsible for the internal affairs of the CCP itself, not least the continuing campaign against personal and institutional corruption. The importance of this institution is illustrated by the fact that both its immediate previous leader (Zhao Leji) and his successor (Li Xi) serve on the Politburo Standing Committee.

Party and state sit alongside one another, but a Party 'hat' is a bigger and better one to have. The state is not, though, simply a shadow or a sham or completely inconsequential.

It is based on the National People's Congress, which, like the National Congress of the CCP itself, meets every five years, approximately four months or so after the main Party conclave. It is rarely in session for more than two weeks and sets the line of travel for the state. It too is extremely sizeable in its membership (there were 2,977 full members in 2023), which, if it is considered to be a parliament (which at least in part it should be), then it is the largest such forum by attendance in the world. It too largely hands down day-to-day activity to another body.

This is a Standing Committee consisting of 175 members. Of these, 116 (two-thirds) are direct nominees of the Communist Party itself. The remainder consist of eight approved minor parties (all of which accept and embrace the 'leading role' of the CCP) and a clutch of independent individuals (who once again are very closely aligned with the CCP). This makes the

Standing Committee the effective legislature with its activities steered by a smaller unit, the Council of Chairpersons. There is a form of internal separation of powers in that members of the Standing Committee should not hold any executive or judicial positions or serve in a wide range of other supervisory roles either.

The National Party Congress has an executive as well as a legislative responsibility. The main organisation is the State Council. This is a substantial institution with oversight of and input from twenty-six ministries, provincial-level governments, the chairs of various commissions, an Auditor-General and such luminaries as the Governor of the People's Bank of China. Its head is the Premier of China, who ranks third after the General Secretary and the State President (who is selected by the National People's Congress every five years, since 2018 without term limits). As these two offices are fused under the leadership of one person and have been for some time, the leader of the State Council/Premier is the number two in the Politburo Standing Committee.

This is not an honorific or nominal position to hold. The Premier is considered to be the person with primary influence over the economy and quite a swathe of domestic political matters. He heads an Executive Body which includes four Vice Premiers and five State Councillors (who have a narrower remit than the Vice Premiers) and a General Secretary. The Premier serves a five-year term in tandem with the National People's Congress but can serve only two terms. Even under a dominant Paramount Leader, the Premier can be a person of serious influence.

Finally, in this rather complicated constitutional apparatus, the NPC is responsible for the Supreme People's Court, the Supreme People's Procuratorate and (since its creation in 2018) the National Supervisory Commission (whose objective is to stamp out corruption in the state). It also has theoretical control over the Central Military Commission of the People's Republic of China (although as the composition of it appears to be identical to that of the Central Military Commission of the Communist Party of China, it is not obvious what this formal power entails).

The crucial point here is that there is a stable institutional framework which even 'core leaders' such as Xi Jinping have little capacity to restructure, other than through an appointment process over which they can have sweeping authority if they retain the confidence of their peers. The Party is manifestly superior to the state, but the state has interests of its own that are distinct and cannot be dismissed entirely even when the Party is (as it has been for more than a decade under Xi Jinping) in an especially assertive mode. This is a more subtle and sophisticated form of political structure than, for example, the one that was established in the heyday of the USSR.

This is reinforced by another inevitable factor in Chinese government and politics. The country is too big and has too large and diverse a population for a full top-down approach to succeed.

There are no less than five separate tiers of administration to deal with. This starts with the provincial level, which includes twenty-one mainland provinces (Taiwan is claimed as well), five autonomous regions (Guangxi, Inner Mongolia, Ningxia, Tibet and Xinjiang), four very large municipalities (Beijing, Chongqing, Shanghai and Tianjin) and the special administrative regions of Hong Kong and Macau. There is then a prefectural level involving 287 designated cities, seven prefectures, thirty autonomous prefectures and three leagues. After that is a county level with 796 districts, 363 county-level cities, 1,347 autonomous counties, forty-nine banners (an Inner Mongolian unit equivalent to a county), three autonomous banners, a special district and a forestry district.

Next, there is a township level which includes 8,096 subdistricts, 20,901 towns, 9,812 townships, two county-controlled districts, 985 ethnic townships, 152 sums (another Inner Mongolian variant) and one ethnic sum. At the base of the pyramid there are still-smaller bodies to deal with, with 99,197 residential committees and 556,425 village committees. As if what has been set out here is not enough of a Rubik's Cube, within these categories there can be exceptions to the broad rule in terms of 'special cases', for instance cities with more of a say in planning and budgetary questions than others that are in the same administrative section. In all of this, the CCP has to staff the relevant institutions with those whom it can recruit to do so. Its ability simply to issue orders and expect a certain outcome is finite. Discretion in implementation will occur. This is also a political structure in which there will be numerous vested, entrenched interests. It reflects a long history of notable local autonomy that is deemed to be the norm in Chinese life.

Party system

It is entirely plausible to assume that the Chinese Communist Party will retain its monopoly on power for the second quarter of the twenty-first century and see in its centenary of national leadership on 1 October 2049. It has been considerably more effective than the old Soviet Communist Party ever was and is acutely aware of the tacit contract it has with the Chinese people: that its standing will not be challenged as long as it delivers material progress.

What sort of Communist Party it will be, however, is much more debateable. One Party does not mean One Outlook, even when the Paramount Leader might appear to hold all the cards in the political deck. The CCP changed orientation dramatically during the Mao era, in the transition from Mao to Deng and since the disciples of Deng (both of Xi Jinping's predecessors as Paramount Leader can fairly be described in that manner) have departed the scene. There is no absolute certainty that the Xi model in its 2017–2022 vintage will continue to be the dominant one in China even if he remains the Paramount Leader for a decade or (although not easy to conceive) even longer. The Party will do what is necessary to best continue to rule in China.

While it would be an overstatement to claim that China is a case of 'One Party, Two Systems', there is clearly a fierce argument over 'market' and 'socialism'. Part of that debate is determined by a sense of what the public will accept. Within weeks of Xi Jinping being returned for a third time as the CCP General Secretary, and hence widely viewed in the West as 'all-powerful' in what was painted as a reversion to the Mao era (always a suspect comparison), his administration felt compelled to abandon the stance of Zero Covid, which had been the hallmark of its approach to that crisis. It did not do so because the evidence surrounding public health provisions, and their effectiveness, had suddenly changed, or been reassessed dramatically. It did so because it was too unpopular.

China is an authoritarian country, but emphatically not a totalitarian one. It has flirted with that semi-Orwellian outcome once before under Mao, and even among Party cadres with the most intense loyalty to the current leader there is no enthusiasm for undertaking that system again. It certainly has the qualities of what can be called a 'surveillance state', but this is in part in order to track signs and causes of discontent, not solely to identify actual and potential dissidents and then deal with them. Although there is censorship aplenty, there is enough social media in existence to make the airing of dissatisfaction inevitable. Moreover, millions of Chinese citizens have now lived, studied and invested overseas. For many, the outside world is a second home, not easily caricatured as the enemy. Individuals can make their own assessments of the credibility of the 'official line'. The importance of a truly huge Chinese diaspora should not be underestimated.

The Party can move in multiple directions. This will play itself out in the short, medium and longer term between 2026 and 2049.

The first stage in affirming its leadership will come with the next National Congress of the CCP, which should take place in late 2027 (and involve the selection of the General Secretary), and then the National People's Congress which is expected to be held in Spring 2028.

The working assumption is that Xi Jinping will want to continue as Paramount Leader. If his health holds, this will probably be the case. If he does, this will not be final proof that he is there as 'leader for life', or that there are no restraints whatever on him or the policies to be adopted.

There are at least three aspects to the CCP politics of 2027/2028 worth inspecting. The first is whether Xi retains all three of his current titles – Party General Secretary, Chairman of the Central Military Commission (with its quirk of being one institution but with two names) and State President – or whether, either to indicate an eventual successor or as a nod to pluralism, the last of these accolades (the most ceremonial and symbolic one) is set to one side, as has previously been seen under CCP rule in China. This is not expected, but not impossible.

The second involves the post of Premier. The past pattern has been for this person to serve two full terms of five years, and then not be a candidate for further advancement but instead take a dignified retirement. A stretch of a decade has been regarded as enough time for appropriate consideration of policy. There has also been a mostly firm (bar the Paramount Leader) informal rule that if a Politburo Standing Committee member has exceeded the age of sixty-seven by the time of a National Congress, then their retirement is obligatory. Li Qiang, the present Premier, will be sixty-eight in mid-2027. Will an exception to the rule be made for him as well? Will this be the justification for a new dictum on age and service to be introduced? Might Li Qiang be shuffled into being President?

The third indicator is what happens to the rest of the Politburo Standing Committee. If the 'sixty-seven in, sixty-eight out' age doctrine is enforced to the letter in 2027, then not only will the Premier have to depart, but the number three (Zhao Leji), number four (Wang Huning), number five (Cai Qi) and number seven (Li Xi) would be obliged to stand down as well. That would leave only Ding Xuexiang (number six), the low-profile Director of the CCP's General Office, in the frame. Is he a conceivable successor or is a jump to a new generation of potential leaders more likely?

Regardless of the short term, some overarching issues will force policy in the years after that.

Societal challenges

The CCP plays with its implicit compact with the Chinese people at its peril and it knows it. Nationalism is not a substitute for material satisfaction. The reincorporation of Taiwan into what Beijing would deem to be the 'mother country' would be a source of genuine satisfaction well beyond the Central Committee of the Communist Party, but not at any price. An increase in military spending which came at the obvious opportunity cost of social expenditure would be a risky roll of the dice. Another bout of the Belt and Road Initiative would not be welcomed.

As chapter 7 set out, the fundamental challenges that China will face between 2026 and 2049 are social and embedded in the near-revolutionary change in the population that will occur. These are not challenges that can be shirked, marginalised or put off for another generation. They will profoundly affect what sort of public might be waving flags and with what level of sincerity when 1 October 2049 arrives. The Party will need to bend towards its public.

These are not incremental obstacles. The population of China is declining, and not because of either a natural disaster as in the past, or a man-made catastrophe such as the Great Leap Forward. The reduction will be slow at the start of the 2026–2049 period, but much more pronounced as the end of that timeframe approaches. The one-child policy may have been abandoned (if not completely repudiated) but the economics of child-rearing as life stands in modern China means that it lives on as a matter of calculation and not compulsion. The sex ratio remains suspiciously skewed a decade after the one-child policy was discarded, and it is difficult to find any explanation other than that in urban as well as rural areas, a proportion of prospective parents actively prefer a male rather than a female child if only one is to be had. This will make for social dynamite, as the number of men who will never marry escalates further.

Those who are born will become part of a society that is ageing rapidly and with a dependency ratio that is destined to decline at an astonishing velocity. This is compounded by a structure for retirement ages which makes no sense in the light of the inevitable demographic changes. It will require incredibly sensitive handling if an increase in the retirement age is not to create social upheaval. Change should have arrived earlier, but it is only beginning to be scheduled and is too minor.

What will the Politburo Standing Committee of the 2030s and 2040s do in response to a social crisis that could mutate into a political crisis? There is only one option on the table, and the issue is when, not if, the CCP shifts to accept this.

China will have to acquire something akin to a social democratic welfare state. The current costs of education, to a degree housing, and healthcare provision, fall heavily on its citizens at the moment, and if this remains the case then it is highly improbable that the fertility rate will improve or that sons and daughters will enjoy equal status universally. There has to be a huge shift in the cost of raising children and that will be at public expense. If it continues to take seven times per capita income to bring up a child (almost double that of the United States and more still than in many nations in Europe) then the status quo will continue. The CCP needs less a Long March than a Quick Dash if demography is not to be a chain.

The same is valid at the other end of the age spectrum. Longer lives are to be applauded. They also need to be prepared for carefully. They are not compatible with retirement ages introduced in an era when many if not most people did not live long enough to reach retirement. The only 'deal' that is out there is one in which significantly later retirement is the norm before 2049, in return for rather more substantial public pension levels than presently available. In some instances, current pensions are close to cursory in what they cover. This cannot carry on.

The CCP will, in other words, need to turn inwards, concentrate on what are incredibly pressing social challenges and be ready to redirect the resources available to it towards social support of several forms. This will also involve asking some tough questions about the existing tax system, with far more people making serious contributions towards income tax than today. The efficiency or not of much provincial, prefectural, county, township and local administrative spending will need to be addressed. This is a seminal shift, yet it cannot be avoided or ignored. As even Xi himself publicly conceded in 2023, there is now a need for 'shifting from primarily regulating quantity to focusing on improving quality, stabilising the total population, optimising the demographic structure, and enhancing population mobility'. It is a massive change that is demanded.

Economic policy

This is because what happens within a society will determine the character of economic policy. China will only avoid the so-called 'middle-income trap' if it can recast the existing model. It will not be able to do that by command alone. It will need to achieve a high level of consent.

China's economic revival has been a marvel to behold, but it is also reaching something of a crossroads. There are some hard facts as it stands – those who lead the CCP in the 2030s and 2040s will need to respond. That cause would be assisted if work started now.

The first hard fact: China has not one economy but two, and arguably three. It has cities and regions among the most dynamic anywhere on Earth, and which are not merely 'developed' but in the highest category of development. Yet there are also large sections of the country that might properly be considered 'developing' and not developed, and which explain why GDP per capita is nowhere near as impressive as overall nominal GDP. And there are vast (admittedly sparsely populated) regions of China which are barely even in a 'developing' form but remain to all intents and purposes 'underdeveloped', hardly touched by the economic transition that Deng initiated and that has continued for decades now.

In the past, there would have been a short-cut available to ameliorate this situation. Many more young people could have been encouraged, and might well not have needed much pressing, to abandon the countryside for the cities. That source of supply is coming close to exhaustion. The numbers left in the countryside are not vast. Many of those who remain are elderly. Besides which, there has to be a minimum agricultural workforce left to feed a country with insufficient arable land.

The second hard fact is that there are ticking timebombs within the economic system that it would be wise for the CCP to defuse, rather than merely hoping that they will not explode. These include a disturbingly high level of debt, much of which is disguised or denied. As almost all debt is held domestically, the shock waves if they came would not be shared with others. The property sector has the capacity to trigger a meltdown across the whole Chinese economy. High unemployment among the millions leaving China's many universities is a danger. There is much in the current economy, despite its undoubted virtues, that has a combustible quality.

The third hard fact is that the state-owned enterprises – riddled as they are with political rather than commercial considerations – severely retard the overall economy. As far back as the 1980s, liberals within the CCP argued that they had to become more independent or be shuttered. There was an element of heresy in that suggestion even then. It would be harder to do now. China was at its most impressive as an economy when the CCP actively fostered the surge in the private sector. This came at the cost of more intense personal and regional inequality, a trade-off that central planning of even the utmost quality would find very difficult to avert. The CCP needs to find a means of letting go of the state-owned enterprises in an orderly manner. The most direct route would be to allow the private sector to expand and to consume them.

The fourth hard fact is the sharp decline in foreign direct investment. The pivot in economic approach, which began in 2013, took time to be appreciated by outsiders, but it has been, and it has led to less confidence among investors that China is a sensible or safe place to put their money. This has been recognised by Li Qiang but only reluctantly (if at all) by his leader. It will take more than putting Jack Ma on a platform to lead to a sense of being open for business.

Finally, the whole concept of the 'crossover' – a date at which China will have surpassed the United States in terms of nominal GDP and consider itself once again (as it has been for so much of its history) the leading economy of the world – may be illusory. If the decrease in its population can be slowed, then it remains entirely possible that a crossover could be recorded well before 2049. The crossover that would really count, that in per capita GDP between China and the US, will not be seen then and possibly never at all.

Foreign policy and national security

The ability of the CCP to adapt itself to these immense social and economic challenges should not be underestimated. At its best, it can function as a form of Chinese National Party, taking all the talents of the nation under its wing, allowing the private sector and civil society more rather than less breathing space and marshalling patriotism in a proactive and positive spirit. It could summon up a strategy that addresses the 'known knowns'. It has shown the capacity in the past to reinvent itself and retain legitimacy.

What it cannot be and succeed as is a Chinese Nationalist (rather than National) Party. Which is what a conflict, or even a Cold War, with the United States would entail for the CCP. This means that three final hard facts come together as a conclusion on China, 2026 to 2049.

The first is that to initiate an outright clash of arms involving an invasion of Taiwan would be utterly reckless. The cost of the enterprise, if it were to be in some way successful (with Taiwan subjugated), in both economic and reputational terms would be astronomical. The price of failure (a military expedition that obviously fell short of what it sought to achieve) would be stratospheric. It makes far more sense for Beijing to deploy a mixture of carrot and stick with Taiwan (depending on which political party is in office there) and play what may have to be an extremely long game.

The second is that any attempt to emulate the United States in terms of military expenditure in either quantity or quality is doomed to failure. The US has a global reach that cannot be anything close to rivalled, and even an effort to be a far closer second place would be ruinously costly. It would come at the sacrifice of expenditure on an essential social transformation at home. It makes more sense to wait and see if the US will continue to want to maintain its global status.

The third is that China may well become a stronger regional player – although with India, Japan, South Korea, the VIPs

(Vietnam, Indonesia and the Philippines) and Australia in contention too, this is not certain. Regional internationalism is likely to be the most that can be achieved, even by 2049. Attempting something more truly global and grandiose is again to court overstretch and failure.

The challenges at home that China will encounter, and the probability of a pragmatic response by the CCP, including edging back in the direction that Deng and his followers favoured, suggest a US–China relationship capable of progress. The Thucydides Trap does not have to be sprung.

13

THE UNITED STATES, 2026–2049

The crystal ball is no clearer for the United States in the second quarter of this century than it is for China. In some ways, as will be indicated here, there is a stronger sense of continuity with the past twenty-five years; in others, the country is arguably more unpredictable than China. It again makes more sense to concentrate on the 'known knowns' first and foremost, recognise a few 'known unknowns' (several can be sought out) and accept the fact that by their very nature, there will be 'unknown unknowns' (especially in terms of potentially transformative technological developments) that are destined to render the most thoughtful of assessments as to what the United States might look like in 2049, and how life will be conducted then, badly flawed.

On the face of it, one might anticipate that the United States and China will follow radically different paths in the quarter-century or so ahead. To a degree, that is a legitimate conclusion. But unexpected similarities might emerge. Like before, the analysis here will focus on five areas or metrics. These are political structure, party system, societal challenges, economic policy and finally, because it is ultimately highly influenced by the preceding four factors, foreign policy and national security. In conducting this enterprise, the words written here will, by implication, if not entirely explicitly, explore whether the American Century has ended, or will have been completed at some point between 2026 and 2049, or may still be a term with relevance beyond the mid-century moment.

Political structure

China is a very old country with a relatively young constitution and political structure (largely dating from 1982). The United States is, by comparison, a very young country with a rather old constitution and political structure (largely dating back to its initial adoption in 1789). This continuity and institutional stability are mainly a source of strength, but they have sizeable side-effects too.

The US Constitution was controversial at the time it was written and involved compromises that did not satisfy everyone (a minority of the delegates who met to deliberate it in 1787 declined to endorse it subsequently or did so with individual caveats). There was sufficient discontent about it that its ratification had to be smoothed by the pledge that a series of amendments would be immediately considered (becoming the first ten such changes or 'Bill of Rights' in 1791). It is the oldest national constitution still functioning anywhere in the world (although predated by the state constitutions of Vermont and Massachusetts). It is relatively short. It has aspects of often intentional ambiguity. It has a very high threshold for amendments (two-thirds of each chamber of Congress and three-quarters of state legislatures). It has the odd howler (on a strict reading, the Vice President would be entitled to preside over their own impeachment trial). It has required the evolution over time of an exceptionally important Supreme Court to serve as an informal standing constitutional modelling service to reconcile the noble words written in the document a very long time ago with the vast number of 'unknown unknowns' that have arrived since the late eighteenth century. This has made not merely the Supreme Court, but the federal judiciary as a whole, immensely controversial and the subject of attempts to influence it. That, for instance, public policy on abortion, notably through *Roe v. Wade* 1973, overturned by *Dobbs v. Jackson Women's Health Organization* 2022, turned on the views of nine judges, is American exceptionalism.

The fundamentals of the political structure thus date to 1789 with the important addition of the Twelfth Amendment endorsed in 1804 which introduced the current system of the election of the President and Vice President as a two-person ticket or team (before then a candidate who received the most electoral college votes became President, the contender who came second the Vice President, a concept with obvious difficulties that did not take long to surface).

The core principle is that of separated institutions sharing powers and thus of checks and balances. The first article of the Constitution created a House of Representatives based on whatever the franchise awarded by individual states might be and a Senate, assumed at the time to be the less significant and more apolitical institution, which would be selected by state legislatures. Laws required the assent of both chambers but were subject to the signature or not of the President (whose veto could be overridden by two-thirds in both houses of Congress). The President would appoint the most important members of the executive, but they would be subject to the approval of the Senate. The President would also nominate members of the US Supreme Court and other federal judicial appointments but with the Senate again involved.

There have only been fifteen amendments since 1804. Some of them relate to the aftermath of the Civil War and the political rights of those who had once been in slavery and servitude. A few extended the franchise as a national right. Prohibition came in (as the Eighteenth Amendment) and then out (as the Twenty-First Amendment). Others were basically tidying-up exercises in practice.

In terms of the structure of politics, only a handful stand out over this long swathe of time. The Sixteenth Amendment (1913) clarified that Congress could levy income tax (vital to the expansion of the role of the federal government thereafter). The Seventeenth Amendment (1913) ensured that Senators would be directly elected in all states (enhancing, over time, the standing of that chamber). The Twentieth Amendment (1933) shortened the transition between presidential terms and when a new Congress would convene. The Twenty-Second Amendment (1951) limited a President to two terms (unless they initially entered the Oval Office towards the end of what would have been their predecessor's term). The Twenty-Fifth Amendment (1967) set out what to do in the event of presidential disability and how to fill the office of Vice President if it were vacant.

To that extent, therefore, it could be argued that the political structure of the United States has an admirable stability to it. Theory and practice can be distant cousins. In reality, electoral outcomes have made for – in both the last quarter of the twentieth century and, especially, the first quarter of this century – something closer to instability, with striking inconsistency in policy as a result.

This can be demonstrated in the following seven observations about recent American politics.

The first is that there has been no dominant party when it comes to the office of the presidency. Taking a fifty-year period from January 1977 to January 2027 (or roughly the post-Mao era in China), the Republicans will have held the White House for twenty-six years, Democrats for twenty-four. In the January 2001 to January 2027 timeframe (approximately overlapping with the tenures of Hu Jintao and then Xi Jinping as Paramount Leader in China), the division of spoils will have been equally even, with Republicans at the executive helm for fourteen years, Democrats for twelve.

The second is that the distinct pattern of presidential elections over the past quarter-century is for the outcome to be close by historical standards either in the popular vote or the electoral college or both. In 2000, George W. Bush lost the popular vote by 0.5 per cent but won in the electoral college (271–267). He was re-elected in 2004, but by a close 2.5 per cent of the popular vote and again a tight margin in the electoral college. Barack Obama was the outlier in 2008, securing a sizeable popular vote lead (7.3 per cent) and a hefty advantage in the electoral college. His popular margin in 2012 was much narrower (3.9 per cent). In 2016 Donald Trump lost the popular vote (by 2.1 per cent) to Hillary Clinton but still managed to prevail in the electoral college. Four years later he lost by a larger margin to Joe Biden (4.4 per cent) but came close to snatching an electoral college majority once again. In 2024 he finally triumphed in the popular vote (by 1.5 per cent) and repeated his electoral college outcome of 2016 (plus Nevada).

What this shows is that the United States has been unusually evenly divided in terms of its presidential vote. The popular vote and electoral college landslides of the past seem over.

The third is that the very even split in terms of party control of the presidency has been duplicated in elections for Congress as well. Over the 1977–2027 period the Democrats have held the House of Representatives for twenty-six years and the Republicans for twenty-four years, although in more recent times (2001–2027) the Republicans have had the upper hand (eighteen years to eight) but in most cases (including as of now) have done so by what have been historically exceptionally small majorities. The Senate over fifty years has been controlled by the Democrats for twenty-five years and eight months and the Republicans for twenty-four years and four months, and from 2001 to 2027 the split will be Democrats thirteen years and eight months, Republicans twelve years and four months (the Republicans held the Senate on a 50/50 split from January 2001 to May 2001 but then one of their number defected to the Democrats, swinging control of that chamber as he crossed the floor). There is no precedent in American political history for control of Congress to be so closely divided.

The fourth is that the results of presidential and mid-term elections since 2000 have strongly favoured 'change' rather than 'continuity' outcomes. In 2000, the presidency changed hands. In 2002, the Senate swapped sides. Continuity occurred in 2004. In 2006, House and Senate reverted to the Democrats. In 2008, the presidency was restored to that Party too. In 2010, Republicans recaptured the House. In 2012, the status quo was endorsed. In 2014, though, normal service was resumed as the Republicans seized the Senate. In 2016, the White House was back in Republican hands. In 2018, the House went over to the Democrats. In 2020, so did the presidency and (on a 50/50 split) the Senate. In 2022, the Republicans (by a very modest margin) took over the House once more. In 2024, the presidency and Senate came to them.

This is a staggering series of elections. Of thirteen contests held every two years from 2000 onwards, eleven have involved some form of partisan shift and a mere two (2004 and 2012) have had continuity. Most observers anticipate that even if Donald Trump is reasonably popular in November 2026, the Democrats will be strongly favoured to retake the House, making it twelve changes out of fourteen.

The consequence of all this for the last quarter-century, fifthly, is that unified party control of the executive and legislative branches from 2001 until the end of the existing congressional term has been the exception. Either split government (the presidency holding one but not both chambers) or outright divided government (the President lacking a majority in either chamber) is the norm. Unified party control has only happened between January and May 2001, from 2003 to 2007 (the longest stretch of this entire age), 2009–2011, 2017–2019, 2021–2023 and 2025– (until 2027?). US Presidents are supposed to have (up to two) four-year terms of office. The recent situation has been for them to have a mere two years of political dominance before their power is diluted.

Another way of putting this, as a sixth point, is that in twenty-five years almost every possible version of partisan control of the key national political institutions has managed to materialise. There can be Republican control of all three of these actors (as seen in 2001, 2003–2007, 2017–2019 and as of today). There can be the Democratic equivalent (2009–2011 and 2021–2023). There can be Republicans with an entirely Democratic Congress (as in 2007–2009) and Democrats with an exclusively Republican Congress (2015–2017). A Republican President could co-exist with a Democratic House and Republican Senate (as Donald Trump did in 2019–2021) or with a Republican House and Democratic Senate (George W. Bush from May 2001 to January 2003). A Democratic President might align with a Republican House and a Senate from his own side (as was the way of Washington DC both in 2011–2015 and during the 2023 to 2025 period).

That leaves one out of eight possible formulations which has not transpired in only twenty-five years, namely a Democratic President serving alongside a Democratic House and with a Republican Senate. That would actually have occurred from 2021 to 2023 if the state of Georgia had not had a run-off election because no candidate won more than half of votes cast at the first time of asking (the Republican took 49.7 per cent in 2020), or if 27,500 voters had switched their vote in that run-off poll. Once again, it is a struggle to locate anything in American political history beforehand that matches our past twenty-five years.

What, finally, does this all mean? The importance of whether a President is accompanied by all, part or none of Congress is, for practical political purposes (particularly domestic legislation), enormous. It is crucial to understand that the seeming certainty to political structure offered by a consistent Constitution is no match for the stunning uncertainty and instability of political outcomes.

On paper, therefore, there have been four individuals who have served as US President since 2001: George W. Bush, Barack Obama, Donald Trump, Joe Biden and Mr Trump once again. This does not seem an excessive number. The reality is that once you take into account whether that President is dealing with a unified, split or absolutely divided Congress then, across twenty-five years, there have been twelve different types of political frameworks (Bush unified 2001, Bush split 2001–2003, Bush unified again 2003–2007, Bush divided 2007–2009, Obama unified 2009–2011, Obama split 2011–2015, Obama divided

2015–2017, Trump unified 2017–2019, Trump split 2019–2021, Biden unified (just about) 2021–2023, Biden split 2023–2025 and Trump back again and unified 2025–). By January 2027, we may well be back to Trump split and a thirteenth presidency.

This has strong implications as we attempt to anticipate the political structure up until 2049. There is no reason to believe that there will be any alteration of the constitutional structure of the United States over the next quarter-century. Separated institutions sharing powers will continue to reign supreme. A power-grab by either the executive or the legislature will falter. This structural stability might offer comfort to some as they contemplate the US in the near future.

The seminal question is whether this is an entirely superficial level of comfort. Are there any respectable arguments as to why there will not continue to be extremely even alteration in party for the position of President, atypically close elections for that office, similarly even division of control in the House and the Senate, a host of change elections, party unified government as the exception rather than the rule, wide variation within the eight possible permutations of command across the executive and the legislature and considerably more presidencies than Presidents? Not many such arguments instantly come to mind. The party system may be responsible for this.

Party system

The United States is likely to maintain a two-party system over the next quarter-century, much as it is a plausible wager that China will retain a single-party system. The barriers to entry for a third party are extremely high and electing not merely a President, but a majority in the House of Representatives and the Senate (especially with staggered elections over six years), for a third party political force would be a massive undertaking. Legal constraints, such as the number of signatures needed for a contender to be on the ballot in many states, are a further deterrent. If the recent instability of the US political structure set out above is troubling, then a viable third party might end up making matters even worse.

Establishing a rival entity to the Democrats and Republicans is not just hard but unnecessary. The primary system, the nature of the media and money make it easier simply to take them over.

This has happened not once but twice in the past quarter-century and will probably be at least attempted, and quite possibly succeed again, in the quarter-century that lies before us.

The first such 'coup' was launched by Barack Obama. It was subtle in that he was an 'insider outsider' who had always been a Democrat and never flirted with an independent run. He was, though, an upstart contender, an insurgent challenger when he announced his candidacy for the Oval Office in February 2007. He had at that stage been a US Senator for a shade over two years (even Jimmy Carter, a one-term ex-Governor of Georgia, had more political experience when he announced for President in 1975). He was emphatically not the preferred choice of his Party establishment (which backed Hillary Clinton), either because he was too unproven or too liberal in his inclinations, or (if not expressed openly) the US was not thought ready for his racial identity.

He won the nomination less because of his performance in the primaries than because he was entirely victorious in those states that held caucuses (where turnout is considerably lower and dominated by those of firm ideological convictions). He started as close to a single-issue figure (his consistent opposition, unlike his main rival, to the Iraq War) but was thrown an extra asset when the US economy came close to collapse under Mr Bush (whose opinion poll ratings even before the global financial crisis struck were desperately dire). His opponent, Senator John McCain, was the best figure that the Republicans could alight on but once the economy tanked and overtook the subjects that were his strength, he was doomed.

The Democratic Party since then has been in many respects the Obama Party. It has more explicitly favoured higher federal government expenditure and in 2009–2011 and 2021–2023 took the chance to legislate for it. It embraces social policy innovation (such as the Patient Protection and Affordable Care Act 2010). It is deeply concerned about climate change. It is culturally progressive (or 'woke' in the vocabulary of its detractors). It is internationalist in its instincts on foreign policy but, like the former President who put more weight on values than interests, is cool about defence spending (which fell sharply as a percentage of GDP from 2009 to 2017), pivoted towards Asia in its strategic thinking (and so sought a meaningful dialogue with China while Mr Obama was in office), is more detached from Israel and focused on world poverty. This is the party system model that Mr Biden and Kamala Harris each inherited and adopted.

The second example, Donald Trump from 2015 onwards, is less of a 'coup' than an act of 'capture', a hostile takeover. Mr Trump was not an 'insider outsider' but an 'outsider outsider'. His party affiliations had been close to promiscuous. He was a registered Republican from 1987 to 1999, then aligned with the Reform Party for two years and tentatively sought out its presidential nomination in 2000, switched to the Democrats in 2001 and remained there until George W. Bush left the Oval

Office in 2009. With Mr Obama now President, Mr Trump went back to the Republicans, hinting in 2011 that he might be available as a presidential champion. When that overture was rebuffed, he reassigned himself as an independent for a short spell and then returned again to the Republicans. Little wonder the Party establishment were wary of him.

Wary or worse they might have continued to be, but they completely lost control of the Party to him. Few senior Republicans thought that he would be their nominee in 2016. Once he was, the widespread calculation was that he would be defeated and that they would be shot of him. Once he emerged the victor, they then sought (with only partial success) to contain him. Once defeated in 2020 they anticipated that he would disappear, whereas he was running again almost immediately, snatched the 2024 nomination with ease and won a second term in office.

Mr Trump has changed the Republicans more emphatically than Mr Obama the Democrats. The Party has acquired what is virtually a cult of personality, with incredibly high approval ratings for Mr Trump among those who identify with his Party. He has pioneered the merits of expanded presidential authority to a party once cautious about that. He has maintained the core of the GOP's economic stance but bolted on tax cuts aimed at lower- and middle-income Americans, tariffs as an explicit form of protectionism and an ambivalence on a high federal budget deficit. He has led the charge for a cultural conservatism that is counter-revolutionary in nature. His foreign policy is led by the Trump doctrine of 'America First', inserting unilateralism and repudiating multilateralism, substantially increasing defence spending while demanding more burden sharing from erstwhile allies and conducting foreign policy as a cost–benefit analysis.

The 'known known' about the American party system in the second quarter of this century is that it is capable of being transformed by individuals determined to make that their mission. The 'known unknowns' are whether what is now the Obama Party and the Trump Party will keep the features of those founders when neither man is on the political scene, the identity of any other individuals who will attempt to emulate them in taking one or other party in a new direction and whether such a person if they emerge will win not just a nomination but assume the presidency.

The societal challenges (and their economic impact) are a matter of somewhat more certainty.

Societal challenges

China faces some excruciating demographic challenges; the United States faces a far softer situation. The latter also has a solution at hand to the difficulties that it might face if it is willing to adjust its approach.

There are numerous demographic studies available, but the one published as the Penn Wharton Budget Model in March 2024 is notably interesting and impressive (with the added twist that Mr Trump is a Wharton alumnus). It sets out a scenario for the US that is testing but not traumatic.

The critical features of its findings are as follows.

The US will not encounter a declining population but one that steadily if perhaps slowly rises. It does not have a crisis with its fertility rate, although it is below the 'magic number' of 2.1. The total fertility rate in 2026 is projected to be 1.7 and stay at essentially the same level in 2049. There is only a very slight difference in the fertility rates of non-college-educated and college-educated women in that timespan and a marginal distinction between the white and non-white fertility rates too.

The racial composition of the country will change between 2026 and 2049 because the size of the various cohorts that reach child-bearing age will alter. The shift is notable but not so stark. By 2049, the percentage of Americans who are white will have declined (to perhaps below 50 per cent), the proportion of African Americans will be up by roughly 30 per cent, the number of Hispanic Americans will have increased by around double that percentage and the Asian American community by over 100 per cent. The United States will certainly be different by mid-century but hardly to an unrecognisable degree.

The study also makes much of the evolving worker–retiree ratio. It compares the numbers of those between the ages of twenty-five and sixty-four and those who are sixty-five and over. It estimates that the ratio which until relatively recently was around 2.9 will fall to 2.55 in 2026 as a result of a large wave of baby boomers reaching retirement, and will continue to edge downwards to 2.29 come 2049. It should, however, be observed that excluding all those between the ages of eighteen and twenty-four from the active workforce appears somewhat excessive and there will be many Americans who reach the age of sixty-five who want to remain in the workforce. The real figure will be higher than 2.29.

If that figure, even if an understatement in practice, is considered to be a matter for concern, then there is an answer awaiting. These statistics assume that the net immigration figures will be similar to those of 2023/2024 and hence be 0.26 per cent in 2026 and stay stable at 0.3 per cent by 2049. If so, then positive immigration would by then not be enough to ensure that the population rises. There could be the threat of a disturbing worker–retiree ratio on the horizon by the mid-century. It would not be the conundrum that China is highly likely to face but it may demand a response.

If the will is there, then that reaction is straightforward. If the immigration rate into the US were around 50 per cent higher (slightly more than a million per year rather than 675,000 individuals), then the 2026 worker–retiree ratio would be maintained in 2049. If a more assertive approach to immigration (such as a 350 per cent increase) is adopted, then the rate would soar back in the vicinity of 3.0. It is hardly the case that there is no room in the United States for more people. What sort of extra people is a fair subject for calm discussion, but the US has a get-out-of-jail-free card to hand.

Economic policy

If the political structure and party system of the United States have an almost anarchic quality to them, then mercifully its economy appears to be oblivious to what can be a chaotic polity. Pessimism about the American economy has been a persistent pastime of pundits for decades. Thankfully, this has not dissuaded entrepreneurs from innovation or the workforce from its toil.

As set out in chapter 8, the case for continued confidence in the US economy is very solid. It is not simply because it has the highest nominal GDP in the world (and may well do in 2049). It is that Americans are, on average, wealthy individuals by international standards. The country has the highest median household income not merely within the G7 but among all OECD member states. The US has the seventh-highest nominal GDP per capita. If one excludes microstates and overt tax havens such as Monaco, Liechtenstein, Bermuda, the Cayman Islands and the Isle of Man, then the only societies richer than the US are obvious atypical cases, countries with far smaller populations that have developed an economic specialism. These are Luxembourg, Ireland, Switzerland, Singapore, Iceland and Norway. With respect, none of these are superpowers.

The other G7 members are some distance back in the rankings. As of 2024, Germany comes in at 17th, the UK at 18th, Canada at 20th, France at 22nd, Italy at 27th and (unexpectedly) Japan is last at 34th. Other economies of some prominence are also a long way behind the American economy: Saudi Arabia at 35th, Russia at number 68, China at 70, Brazil at 80 and India at a lowly 136th. The US is not set to become relatively impoverished as it moves between the years 2026 and 2049.

This is because the basic building blocks of its economy are close to uniquely advantageous. It is a high productivity economy (stretching its lead of late) with a modern infrastructure for transportation, extensive natural resources (including being the leading global producer of petroleum and natural gas), a giant hub of venture capital and research and development expenditure and medical innovation, and a private sector that is 85 per cent of the economy. It does have a historical high debt-to-GDP figure (although nothing like the headache for Beijing), severe income inequality and a battered manufacturing base, but it will stay king of the castle. Political structures and a warped party system have proven no match for its economic prowess. Even if a notional crossover between the US and China were to occur some years before 2049, it would not mean that the US had ceased to be the most significant developed economy by far.

Foreign policy and national security

The United States has been living through more complex times of late. From about 1990 to 2015 (the 'Great Moderation'), it was the exclusive example of an economic, political, military, technological and cultural superpower. This has been interrupted and displaced by an altogether more disruptive era (the 'Great Fragmentation'). This has perhaps undermined confidence in some elite American circles and fuelled the fear that China is more than a competitor or even a rival, but an existential threat.

A few deep breaths should afford some perspective. The United States has, if it wants to retain it, an influence on international politics that far exceeds any other player and will do so in the second quarter of this century. It has a global reach in terms of military assets that has no credible competition. It will soon be spending as much money on defence as the next ten nations combined (including China) can muster. It has cultural clout (even if Mr Trump is not flavour of the month in many other places overseas) that no other nation can emulate. It is home to some extraordinary technology companies and will doubtless foster many more in the decades to come. It is not about to be undermined by a demographic challenge that requires an enormous redistribution of resources to counter. Its economy will not implode. The American Century cannot be said to have ended. It could even continue all the way to 2049.

The real dilemma in American foreign policy and national security is a continuation of a very old one, set out in chapter 2. It remains the only 'ism': a nation that thinks of itself as an idea as well as a geographical entity. What balance does it want to strike between its 'monastic' and 'missionary' traditions? Within those strains, there are different options available. Is

'America First' more of a return to the ethos of Theodore Roosevelt, or the mindset of a Thomas Jefferson or James Monroe? Back in 1991, Wang Huning, now the main ideologist of the CCP and number four on the Politburo Standing Committee, the most important political body in China, published a book on his six-month 1988 stint in the US entitled *America Against America*. In a sense, he was right and ahead of his time.

14

PATH TO PEACE

Conflict, even an outright clash of forces, between China and the United States is not inevitable, or unavoidable, or even more likely than not at some point from 2026 to 2049. The two nations should not be regarded as 'destined for war'. If there is a Thucydides Trap, then it is an intellectual one. It is the risk of assuming that a certain sort of interpretation of the past (a particularly distant past in this instance) can in some way predetermine the future. It cannot. There is instead the danger that this outlook becomes the father of a self-fulfilling prophecy.

If China and the United States come anywhere close to blows, it is more likely to be the result of accident rather than design. There have been far too many examples of this in human history to dismiss the possibility out of hand. It is the most likely source of a rupture. Action should be taken to minimise it.

This is an even more relevant challenge because of the uncertain nature of the new geopolitics. The Cold War was hardly an appealing spectacle, with the real prospect of nuclear annihilation for much of the planet if the leadership of one or other (or both) of the superpowers were to make a massive miscalculation or fail to recognise reckless brinkmanship. It was, despite or because of the menace of Mutually Assured Destruction, nonetheless, a geopolitical order. It was conducted through bilateral deliberations on a periodic basis; there was an institutional architecture to it, and there were tacit understandings that approached the status of rules. This was of real value in the 1989–1991 period when, almost out of nowhere, the Berlin Wall fell, other East European countries embraced democracy, the Warsaw Pact as a military organisation collapsed, West and East Germany became fused as one country once more, and the USSR itself was dissolved.

American leadership in these years was skilful, and neither George H.W. Bush nor James Baker III, his Secretary of State, has perhaps received the accolade and appreciation they deserved, but they were assisted by the fact that there was a tool kit which they could work with. This was not entirely an episode of improvisation and innovation. There were formal mechanisms as well. The transition from a Cold War order to a post-Cold War one was, looking back, a smooth affair.

The twenty-five years or so of that immediate post-Cold War order (approximately 1990–2015) also had the fundamental features of an order. What would be dubbed the 'Great Moderation' had three core components which were widely understood (if not necessarily universally liked) by the vast majority of states and governments. The first was that the United States was much more than first among equals. It was the single economic, political, military, technological and cultural superpower in existence. The second factor was that the overall international economic environment was broadly benign, in that inflation was a word that existed in dictionaries but not in advanced economies, with central banks individually and collectively having mastered it. The third was that trade across borders was surging in what was termed 'globalisation'. It always had some critics, but it had become economic orthodoxy. This had been assisted by the intelligent incorporation of China into the global economy, which was seen to be a positive event for the country and its enormous population and for the world as a whole. These twenty-five years were not paradise but, yet again, had tacit understandings that approached the status of rules.

They did, though, in retrospect include what might be considered a serious missed opportunity. There was no wholesale exercise in which it was asked whether the main global institutions that had either been set up at the conclusion of and in the aftermath of the Second World War, or that had been set up during (and significantly shaped by) the Cold War, were truly fit for purpose after 1990. If they were adapted or amended at all, it was incremental. Institutional invention was not there.

The age in which we live now – which I have called the 'Great Fragmentation', but there are many other designations that could be deployed – is very different. It is better defined by what it is not than what it actually is. There is hard evidence that all three of the old key features are not with us any longer. The absolute supremacy of the United States, even though it remains much more than a first among equals, is not an unchallenged assumption. Inflation, in many ways triggered by a global pandemic and its aftershocks which were entirely unexpected, has made its return, and while it appears to have peaked in most places, it has not been suppressed entirely. Globalisation is grounded. Protectionism is popular. The old religion of free trade lacks friends. There is no post-post-Cold War structure or order to speak of, nor have many new ideas for one been put forward. There are not the tacit understandings that approach the status of rules.

Which means that the United States and China are vulnerable to becoming the victims of a void. The geopolitics of the jungle is not the place to be. The absence of sufficiently robust and, at least as important, sufficiently relevant institutional arrangements involving the US and China makes accidental antagonism between Washington and Beijing an acute danger. The status quo may be a slippery slope.

It is, therefore, not merely in the mutual interests of the United States and China to find better means to explain themselves to one another but in the overall interests of international relations. An enhanced US–China dialogue not only makes peace a better prospect than conflict, it is the foundation for attempting to find a new structure, order, tacit understandings, and even rules.

The remainder of this chapter sets out the sort of changes to consider.

Revive (but rebrand) the notion of the 'G2'

In a far-sighted act of thinking, the Obama administration floated the notion of a 'G2' initiative. It came early in Xi Jinping's tenure, and he responded coolly. Although he was looking for a different kind of great power arrangement at the time, he also saw China as the leader of the developing world as much as, perhaps more than, the developed one. The idea was extinguished due to a lack of shared enthusiasm. It has not been touched again.

It should be revived but rebranded ('G2' has an almost imperial smack to it). At its centrepiece should be a commitment to an annual summit between the leaders of the two nations as a fixed aspect of the international diplomatic calendar, with each country taking it in turns to host.

These should not be the sorts of summits that involve cannons being fired on lawns, guards being inspected, relatively short formal meetings, bland communiqués agreed before a word has been spoken and state dinners of many courses and an extraordinary amount of cutlery. This is more likely to spark one-upmanship than anything more enlightened and informative.

A better formula would be the one that was devised for the first official working meeting between Barack Obama and Xi Jinping in June 2013 at the Annenberg Retreat at Sunnylands in Rancho Mirage, California. This was, by the standards of these matters, extended in duration (there would be no harm in adding another day for deliberations), largely informal and secluded. It was a private opportunity for each side to present its positions and concerns to the other, and through that process identify where there were openings for constructive engagement. It made it easier to escape the dead ends of arguments about areas such as US arms sales to Taiwan or China's approach to the Uyghurs, which would involve much more heat than light. A by-product of the Sunnylands conversation was that, for the rest of the Obama era, even when the atmosphere between the countries was relatively fractious, it was possible to find a method for working together on climate change, where each leader saw merit in interacting with the other. Annual summits of this kind will not always 'clear the air' but they beat megaphone diplomacy. The case for formalising such an arrangement is forceful. It requires someone to move first.

Create a US–China Co-operation Council

A deep and meaningful conversation held every twelve months is a sound start, but it requires something akin to a secretariat in order to maintain its momentum. This is not a task for two leaders alone. Imaginative institutional invention would put some flesh on the political bones. It would also allow a focus on the issues most likely to disrupt the relationship.

An option would be to establish a US–China Co-operation Council. It could consist of the two respective chiefs of staff to the President and the General Secretary, and (realistically allowing for the schedules of their superiors) a dedicated Assistant Secretary at the State Department, Treasury, Department of Defense and Department of Commerce for the United States and their counterparts within China (who will exist within the State Council of the National People's Congress). Other figures could be invited as circumstances required.

A Council of this form would keep the bilateral relationship on track between annual summits. It might meet in official session between two and four times a year (quarterly, but not when that coincided with the annual summit might be about the right format). Personal contacts would be formed which would make it more straightforward to talk either as a whole or between, say, the Assistant Secretary at the US Treasury and his Chinese equivalent if there were shocks, or the chance of shocks, that would have an impact not only on China and the United States but the entire global economy. An institutional sounding board to avoid a dialogue of the deaf. A small secretariat would assist in the effectiveness of this organisation. It is worth the experiment.

A link between Congress and the National People's Congress

As the US Congress is a serious force in American foreign policy (and can be a source of tension particularly when one or other, or especially both, chambers are politically hostile to the

President), it would be a mistake to exclude it from institutional innovation. In a system of separated institutions sharing powers, Congress is part of the American government; it does not merely hold it to account as would be the case for many European parliaments. The words and deeds of its leading figures can have an impact on the wider US–China relationship. Any doubt in this regard surely ceased when the visit of Nancy Pelosi, then the Speaker of the US House of Representatives, to Taiwan led to loud and seemingly sincere shouts of disapproval in Beijing (probably because it was assumed that she must have made the trip at the behest of, or at least with the blessing of, President Biden). Congress needs to be part of a path to peace.

Exactly how this is to be achieved is more taxing to envisage. It would need to be a far looser arrangement than that of the US–China Co-operation Council outlined previously. An informal joint committee of the House and Senate with the Standing Committee of the National People's Congress (which is the functional legislature in China on a day-to-day basis) would provide a base and there could be mileage in figures on both sides being invited to observe proceedings (private as well as public) within Congress and the full NPC when it assembles. As many a Member of Congress has entered the executive as President, Vice President or Cabinet member, and a similar career path can be seen in the NPC Standing Committee in China, this would be more than a 'talking shop' but a chance to make contacts between those destined to rise higher.

Start work on a US–China Fair Trade Accord

Trade has become established as a very large thorn in the side of the US–China relationship. It became an irritant towards the end of the Obama White House as dissatisfaction with not only the size of the bilateral trade deficit but the tactics that the Chinese government allegedly adopted to entrench its advantage multiplied. It burst into the open from 2018 to 2020 when the Trump administration flexed its muscles and imposed more than $350 billion worth of tariffs on China which led to an (entirely predictable) tit-for-tat reaction from Xi Jinping that bruised both sides before, after more than one false start, a truce of a kind was established again in 2020.

The Biden administration did not reverse that Trump approach wholesale. It was more open to protectionist pressures than either the Clinton or the Obama presidency had been. The secret (insofar as it was remotely suppressed) to Mr Biden's victory in 2020 had been narrow wins in Michigan, Pennsylvania and Wisconsin, states where the manufacturing base had eroded over decades with China seen as the beneficiary and the catalyst of its decline. Mr Biden was viewed as a more credible defender of its interests than Mrs Clinton conveyed the impression of being. This allowed him to beat Mr Trump in 2020. He had no intention of allowing that sense of personal commitment on trade to be dissipated.

The Republicans, and Mr Trump himself, were not about to be outflanked on trade policy and in opposition hardened their stance on China considerably. The Party platform adopted at its national convention in 2024 stated bluntly, in a section named 'Protect American Workers and Farmers from Unfair Trade', that 'Republicans will revoke China's Most Favored Nation status, phase out imports of essential goods and stop China from buying American Real Estate and Industries'. If that strategy were to be followed, US–China trade would be dramatically lower. When a new tariff war broke out in the aftermath of his 'Liberation Day' announcements in April 2025, with tariff rates imposed on China swiftly reaching an incredible 145 per cent before being scaled back, only for more discontent to emanate from the White House again, it appeared as if trade really could become the disagreement that made the whole relationship untenable.

The twists and turns of tariffs and trade across the whole Trump second term are yet to come. The possibility that what might start life as a negotiating position evolves into a philosophical reorientation is real. Both sides might decline to blink (although there have clearly been some backchannels between them throughout the public disharmony). Diplomacy and economics should be capable of an element of separation. Yet a contagion effect can take place here too.

There needs to be a search for more than a semblance of a ceasefire, which will not hold with any resilience. The bigger picture on trade needs to be addressed, and urgently.

The United States, and notably President Trump, considers itself open to a 'big, beautiful deal'. A bargain of any credibility would be better than the trading version of a contest of attrition. The shape of such an outcome has, however, to reflect the realities of what is a highly political fight.

The idea of some form of US–China Free Trade Agreement is fanciful. The two sides are much too far apart and the Republican appetite for the very words 'free trade' is not what it was in the Reagan era, or even under George W. Bush. It would take years to negotiate, almost certainly stall with fingers pointed at one another, and hence as an exercise might do more harm than good. Something more limited but practical is required.

That could come via a more forensic and targeted US–China Fair Trade Accord rather than an ambitious, expansive and wildly optimistic US–China Free Trade Agreement. It would focus on the main bones of contention and be more about opening up what can be an unofficially closed Chinese market to aspiring American exporters than shutting out mainstream Chinese exports from US consumers who would otherwise be inclined to acquire them. The way to reduce the deficit would be by levelling up on the American side, not clamping down on the Chinese camp. This would in turn allow the pledge to 'revoke China's Most Favored Nation status', which would be incredibly destructive if it were delivered, to be quietly mothballed. Without some activism here, the United States and China will find themselves in mutual lose-lose terrain.

The four proposals above are in essence about the bilateral and inter-governmental relations between the United States and China. There is a large role for wider civil society to play too.

Academic and intellectual exchange

Cities, towns and even villages in North America, Europe and elsewhere have long engaged in 'twinning', forming an association with such locations beyond their shores, either because there is a historical link between them, or they share certain similarities, or a matter of chance where a local notable takes a shine to such an alliance and convinces others to back it as well.

A similar but perhaps more structured process between universities in the US and China, the think-tanks that exist in both countries and private endowments and foundations (of which there are a few of note in China as well as a more sizeable number within the United States) might well provide dividends. China has long been fascinated by the US (for a variety of reasons). The same cannot be asserted of those at the centre of American academic and intellectual life. Mutual understanding would be served by establishing institutional links and fostering many more exchanges (with a premium on Americans familiarising themselves with East Asia). As in so many spheres, this is about serious leadership. A Kennedy School of Government, Brookings Institution or Carnegie Endowment for International Peace has to move first, even creating a physical outpost in China if that is permissible and practical to do (as it should be). Others would follow if a lead were to be taken.

Super-sized student scholarships

Among the many areas of international life where the United States and China rank first and second in the world is in the number of billionaires. According to the 2025 analysis by *Forbes*, the United States has 902 such individuals and China some 450 (Mao must be turning in his grave). This is an imprecise area of detection and there may well be secretive individuals and families in both countries who have evaded the best efforts of highly trained wealth hunters. That there is a lot of money in these bank accounts and family offices cannot be disputed.

Many of these people are proven philanthropists or could be inspired to become one for the right cause. There are, of course, many extremely worthy causes to which cash can be donated and there are some high-profile Americans who have already announced that they intend to distribute a very large percentage of what they currently hold before reaching the end of life.

What would be among the best contributions that they could make to the world? There is a robust case to be offered that the creation of a new set of student scholarships for educating young Americans in China and young Chinese people in the US would be a fantastic investment in the promotion of peace and understanding. This would ideally be of a scale that far exceeds anything that has happened before. It would be a moon shot of minds. It would be a bequest to the future of both countries over the next quarter-century and beyond.

It is not an insanely idealistic suggestion, nor would it be impractical to organise. Billionaires in the United States tend to move in similar circles and will already have co-operated with each other in supporting causes that they consider important, be that in education or across the arts. One suspects that much the same is true in China.

Once more this is about leadership, but by an elite section of private citizens and not politicians. There is already a compelling prototype in the Stephen A. Schwarzman scholarships for American students at Tsinghua University in Beijing. He should not be flying almost solo with such an initiative.

A band of American billionaires needs to come together and co-ordinate, albeit informally, with Chinese figures of the same standing. It would take only one prominent individual to put their hand up (and the other hand in their pocket) for the project to become viable. The optimal outcome would be a fund jointly established by billionaires in the United States and China. The (Elon) Musk–(Jack) Ma scholarship scheme might be far-fetched, but there are other figures who could make the initial contribution and allow a programme to get off the ground in the 2020s.

This will doubtless be opposed by some who will cite concerns of espionage or indoctrination. They must not be allowed a veto. Student scholarships have been a benign form of 'soft power' in many contexts and sectors. The path to peace would be enhanced if an initiative of vast inclusion and reach allowed massively more young people to experience the two societies.

Corporate collaboration

A new Cold War, or worse still, outright military hostilities, between the United States and China would do few favours to the corporate communities in either country (with the fledgling private sector in China potentially particularly exposed). Business has a shared interest in peace. Even the arms industry would prefer that its products were not activated in anger in a contest between Washington and Beijing. Less drastically, total trade wars with the demand for the decoupling of the two economies, while not as bad as bombs and bullets, would not be welcomed in boardrooms across the US and China either. All too often, despite this, business seems to be a bystander, only making itself heard, or trying to do so, when emergencies strike.

The institutional relationship between corporate America and corporate China is not especially well developed. Contacts at a personal level appear to be infrequent and rarely co-ordinated. There is an array of business councils out there (some of which do sterling work, and which have strived to be vehicles for better and broader mutual understanding) and conferences are conducted, but these tend to be sectoral rather than strategic in their orientation. Businesses in China and the United States are not exactly strangers but can be passing acquaintances. As the two nations are responsible for more than 40 per cent of world GDP, this is not a close enough link.

A 'big bang' approach is needed over the next quarter-century. The notion should be that of a US–China Economic Forum, which takes the existing World Economic Forum as its model but adapts it to allow for annual meetings (alternating between the countries) and intervening activities organised around types of economic output or the professional services engaged in. Many of the biggest names in Chinese business – Baidu, Alibaba and Tencent – are barely known in the US, let alone recent younger upstarts like Meituan and Pinduoduo. Ignorance is rarely bliss when it comes to the business landscape. There would be enormous advantages to the corporate communities of the United States and China becoming vastly more familiar with each other and acting as a force for quiet dialogue.

Address artificial intelligence urgently

The need to talk is at its most intense in the frontier territory that is artificial intelligence. There is the seminal risk that rivalry between firms such as OpenAI and DeepSeek (and others yet to obtain a profile) will blind them to the consequences of what it is that they are exploring and what the effects and implications could be for human society. The two governments may be bewitched into not asking questions, nor regulating the space too closely. They may come to regret this. We may all discover that artificial intelligence should have come with more thought.

This has at least been acknowledged by China. In July 2025, at the World Artificial Intelligence Conference in Shanghai, Li Qiang, China's Premier, proposed establishing an organisation to foster global co-operation on AI. This is not a notion that should be simply dismissed out of hand.

The final set of proactive moves on the path to peace have to arrive through international action. In all three cases, this will not be forthcoming unless the United States chooses to take a lead.

China should enter the G7 (and be a full member of the OECD)

The G7 is a classic example of an important international institution that was created during the Cold War and influenced in its form by that titanic struggle, but which has not considered the role that it should aspire to during the post-Cold War age, never mind the post-post-Cold War of now. Its membership was formed in a series of steps in the 1970s, starting informally with the US, West Germany, France and the United Kingdom, with Japan then added, a little later Italy, and Canada to enhance the North American contingent and because it had a well-established Prime Minister (Pierre Trudeau). The UK which acted as the host in 1978 invited the (British) President of the European Commission along and it remains a full participant (if not quite a truly full member).

The only change made after this was to include Russia in 1998 (which made little sense as it was an economic basket case). Moscow was expelled in 2014 after the Russian invasion of Crimea.

It is a nonsense that China as the second-largest economy in the world and indeed India as the fourth were not invited into the fold some considerable time ago. This should also have been the moment when the G7/G8/G9 professionalised itself further, obtaining a permanent secretariat, a formal base and a bespoke budget to examine issues of international concern (the previously highlighted sector of artificial intelligence would be exactly the right type).

Instead, inertia has led to a weakening of that which the G7 was supposed to strengthen. In 2009, BRIC (Brazil, Russia, India and China) was born. Shortly after entered South Africa. In the quest to be larger still, but at the cost of any kind of economic coherence, in 2024 invitations were issued to Egypt, Ethiopia, Iran and the United Arab Emirates (what they have in common is not obvious) and in 2025 Indonesia found itself inside the tent as well. It is hard to conceive that this BRICS+ would be abandoned outright even if China and India were incorporated into a G9 tomorrow (as they should be). The damage would at least be belatedly limited if they came in.

One additional slight should also be corrected. The OECD, founded again in the Cold War age in 1961, is an institution of substance, with a proper staff, a base in Paris and funds for investigations. It has today thirty-eight members; neither Beijing nor New Delhi are full members of the club but only have the standing of 'participating partners'. So, Costa Rica is in, but China is out. The Isle of Man as a UK dependent territory is technically in, India is out. This is no way to treat either country.

Allow China to participate at its due weight in the IMF and the World Bank

China is not shut out from the International Monetary Fund (IMF) or from the World Bank (the combination of the International Bank for Reconstruction and Development [IBRD] and the International Development Association [IDA]) or from the wider World Bank Group (which involves the International Finance Corporation, the International Centre for Settlement of Investment Disputes and the Multilateral Investment Guarantee Agency). This is an improvement on its exclusion from the G7 and its comparatively minor position in the OECD.

This is an accident of history. The IMF and the World Bank were both devised in 1944 and came into existence in late 1945, under the parentage of the United Nations which had itself just been created. China was then under the leadership of the Nationalists and the United States very much wanted it to be included (as it also pressed for the country to become a permanent member of the UN Security Council). If the IMF and the World Bank had not been established until 1955, China may well have been out. As it was, it was only in 1980 that Taiwan had to make way for the People's Republic of China, nine full years after that transition had been authorised in the UN itself. These are very important institutions. The IMF is financed by 191 members. The World Bank overall has 189 states represented within it (with 175 of them inside the IDA).

So, China is in but its authority and voting weight do not reflect the size of its economy. In the IMF it has a voting share that is less than 40 per cent of that of the United States and is slightly less than that of Japan. In the IBRD (which is the critical lending arm of the World Bank), China has less than a third of the voting entitlement of the United States and a somewhat lower share than Japan. Hardly for the first time, international institutions that arrived in one age (the pre-Cold War in these instances) have not been adequately adjusted to the post-post Cold War arena. When China senses that it is not being awarded the amount of respect that it is entitled to, then, just as with what has become the BRICS+, it will find an alternative to enhance its status. In 2015, it set up the Asian Infrastructure Investment Bank which looks like a rival to the World Bank.

The path to peace might be long and meandering but it is not a road to nowhere. It is entirely possible to incorporate China into the quarter-century that starts in 2026 as much as a partner to the United States as a rival, and with managed competition, not conflict, the order of the day. Apathy and indifference are the real enemies of this outcome. The programme for a path to peace articulated here is by no means exclusive or exhaustive, nor is it the only prospectus out there. Whatever strategy is adopted will require leadership in the public and private domains. Yet, as the Chinese saying has it, 'a journey of a thousand miles begins with a single step'.

Conclusion:

THE ARISTOTLE ANSWER

It is not enough to win a war; it is more important to organise the peace.

Aristotle

What should one conclude then about the nature of the relationship between China and the United States in the approximately quarter-century that will pass between 2026 and 2049?

China and the United States are very different countries. If one accepts that China has been a continuous civilisation for around 5,000 years, then the United States has only existed for 5 per cent of that timespan. If one is a little less romantic and dates China as a consistent concept back a mere 2,500 years (which might not make one popular in certain circles) then it becomes 10 per cent. This alone is significant. As argued at the outset, it is fundamental to understanding how China and the United States view themselves and their place in the wider world: that one sees itself as the custodian of a civilisation and the other regards itself as being, uniquely, an 'ism', an idea or even an ideology as well as a nation.

There is nothing that is remotely combustible about this state of affairs, nor does it innately suggest that a contest or even a conflict between the two countries is disproportionately likely. It is, though, a potential source of elementary mutual miscomprehension if not properly grasped.

Their history parts company in three other respects. China has spent much of its many centuries struggling to acquire and maintain consistent and stable borders. The United States has not. Whether by acquisition or annexation it has been secure within its boundaries for the overwhelming majority of its existence. The most serious test of whether this would hold true was not the consequence of an external invasion but an internal military confrontation, the US Civil War. This might have led to a division into two different nations. It did not. The Union was retained.

At about the same time, China was entering the downwards spiral that would become its One Hundred Years of Humiliation, a dire decline that would grow worse by the last decade of the nineteenth century and verged on the terminal (for the ruling dynasty) by the first decade of the twentieth. At around this point, the United States was about to enter the American Century, an episode in its history which in many ways has probably not yet drawn to a close.

Finally, the 1940s were years of incredible importance for both the United States and China. For the US it was entry into the Second World War, engagement on a far more massive scale than was the case in 1917–1918, victory in Europe and Asia, becoming the first nuclear weapons state and a superpower. For China it was an end to foreign occupation, the close of civil war and the victory of the CCP.

History has a sibling in geography (which field of study is the older of the two or the more important is a matter for intense debate and dispute). At one level, China and the (continental) United States are really quite similar not only in their size but also as to where in the Northern Hemisphere they sit. The critical distinction is that while the United States has long been blessed by a large supply of arable land, China has not. Feeding a substantial proportion of humanity has always been (and to a degree remains) the first test of leadership, whether those at the helm are awarded the title of King or Emperor or General Secretary of the Chinese Communist Party.

The second observation is that the historical engagement between the two countries has been a rollercoaster. The experience started with something approaching awe on the American side but slid into a state that verged on outright contempt during the depths of China's One Hundred Years of Humiliation, and then saw empathy revived during the FDR presidency, with Japan viewed as the unambiguous villain in its dealings with China and with the Chinese people themselves.

If anything, this would be the catalyst for an unfortunate element of innocence in American thinking about China once the two became overt allies after 1941. The argument was loudly articulated that the two nations were natural allies whose similarities were such that the alliance would last long after Germany and Japan had been defeated (which explains why the US was so determined that China should be treated as a full war victor and must acquire a permanent seat at the United Nations Security Council to be established once the war ended). The media coverage of Chiang Kai-Shek and Madame Chiang in the United States was fawning. She took part in a triumphant tour of the US in 1942–1943 including an address made to Congress. As the eminent historian of American foreign policy, Robert Dallek, put it in *The American Style of*

Foreign Policy: 'In the immediate post-war period, Americans remained hopeful that China might still evolve into an East Asian United States.' All of which made October 1949 hurt more.

So, infatuation was rapidly abandoned for disengagement and the implausible proposition that Taiwan was the seat of the real administration of China and the authorities in Beijing illegitimate. For almost twenty-five years, the United States and the China of Chairman Mao had little if anything to do with one another. This would change in spectacular fashion with Richard Nixon's visit in 1972, which would lead before the 1970s were out to formal US recognition of Red China.

The forty-five years or so since have seen the relationship become at times closer and then once again more distant. The 1980s saw Washington champion the Deng experiment until the use of force in Tiananmen Square plunged bilateral ties into frozen territory. There would be a recovery in the 1990s with the Clinton administration eventually determining to be a cheerleader for closer ties. Matters were broadly amicable in the years when George W. Bush and Barack Obama were the occupants of the White House. Since then, tensions (often deep) have become the norm.

The United States and China are likely to remain very different countries in the 2026–2049 era.

They will have fundamentally distinct challenges in terms of their societies because dilemmas involving their demography are so diverse. China will face a declining population (albeit slowly at first), a fertility rate that is well below the replacement rate and without the realistic chance that mass immigration might be a salvation, the risk of a continuation of a skewed gender ratio, a very rapidly ageing population and a disturbingly low figure for the balance between those who have left the active workforce and those who are still in it and have to support those outside it. The US will encounter nothing of the same scale and can reach for the immigration lever if it has the political will to pull it. Its main social conundrum is how best to manage what will over time be a changing racial composition (with the spurt in Asian Americans likely to be a strong aspect) but this has been true, if not at the same intensity, for much of the past quarter-century as well.

The economies of China and the US cannot avoid the gravitational forces of social evolution. The principal challenge for China will continue to be how best to manage being both a developed economy and (for some years to come) a developing one, with the aim that by 2049 (a credible target), China will be an overwhelmingly developed economy, one perhaps with the highest nominal GDP on the planet and with far less of a chasm between its GDP per head and those of other developed nations, never mind the United States, that exists today. The preoccupation for the United States should not be the underlying vitality of its core economy. Its main challenge may come from artificial intelligence transforming it into a hyper-developed economy at an unexpected speed and with profound social consequences.

All of this has implications for foreign policy and for national security. The United States will have the tools that it needs in the second quarter of this century to remain an economic, political, military, technological and cultural superpower, if not with the outright monopoly of assets and ambition that it enjoyed during the decades of the 'Great Moderation' (c.1990–2015). It will not be displaced by another or a collection of others as the actor with the most extensive and impressive global reach. Technology may even extend its position. The real issue is not what the United States *can* be in the international system, but what it *wants* to be.

China, even by mid-century, will focus on being the most significant player in its region. It will have global aspirations, but not the resources needed to take that charge up and to the full.

Within this overall framework there will be unanticipated curiosities.

In the case of China, it is that its political structure is, relative to the United States, young and has a single-party system that looks comparatively anomalous (illiberal democracies may appear to be on the march in the 2020s but the imposition of a one-party state through them has not materialised, even if the quality of those democratic polities might have declined). Yet it is stable.

Stability does not exclude change. It is also not outrageous to speculate that the CCP after the end of the tenure of Xi Jinping, due to social and economic challenges that the Party must address as much as anything else, will edge back in a direction somewhat closer to that identified with Deng and his disciples. The balance between 'market' and 'socialism' can shift once again. The political elasticity of the CCP should not be underestimated. It is more probable than not that it will prove to be the China National Party, not the China Nationalist Party.

While its political structure and party system might be rigorous, robust and relatively reliable, its society and economy are far less straightforward for its political elites to contain or to control. It is much more probable that these social and economic factors will dictate political decisions to be taken, rather than the other way round. Transformational technology could be an even harder earthquake to deal with within China than it might prove for the United States of America.

The logic of all this is that any drive for guns over butter in China is a quest that courts failure. China plays a long game and rarely takes reckless risks of its own volition. That will remain true.

Thinking about the United States over the next quarter-century produces different conclusions which, in essence, are close to the opposite of those that might be tentatively made on China.

As asserted in chapter 13, the United States has a political structure and party system that in theory should be expected to be more stable than those of China ... but are not in reality. The political structure, when combined with the electoral outcomes of the past twenty-five years, has been the cause of inconsistency, instability and occasional incoherence in the application of US policy. Party control of the White House has been split extremely evenly; the recent trend has been for the results for that office to be very close by historical standards, the House of Representatives and the Senate have been similarly intense political battlegrounds, 'change elections' have been all the rage, unified partisan control of Washington occurs less frequently than either split or outright divided government, and seven out of eight possible combinations of party composition in the White House and Congress have been witnessed in little over two decades (with the last one narrowly missed in 2020). A small number of presidents but a large array of presidencies. There are few reasons to think that these features of the system will not be there in 2026–2049.

In a similar vein, the party system of the United States has evolved in an unanticipated manner. The United States has had a de facto two-party system for about 160 years since the Civil War (or around twice the length of time that China has had single-party CCP rule). Many of the major dividing issues have remained the same across time (some of them, including attitudes to the appropriate role of the United States in international affairs, stretch all the way back to 1776), but the parties have moved across the spectrum in their stance on these matters. Republicans were once the most liberal on civil rights but reverted towards states' rights in later decades. The Democrats made the reverse political voyage. At varying moments one or other of the parties has been the more or the less protectionist, the more or the less in favour of activist government (whether this be through cuts in taxation or a substantial increase in federal spending), the more or the less determined to reverse a perceived decline in the manufacturing base of the US. The two-party system has allowed for considerable philosophical flexibility throughout history.

In one sense, the party system has become more consistent and coherent. Some fifty years ago, one could still speak of 'conservative Democrats' and 'liberal Republicans' as distinctive factions in Congress. Liberal Republicans could and would endorse the agenda of Lyndon Johnson. The conservative Democrats provided the critical votes in the House of Representatives to enact Ronald Reagan's tax-cutting blueprint. In foreign policy, politics often stopped 'at the water's edge'. This was less true by the start of the twenty-first century. It had almost totally disappeared at the second quarter of that century. The Republicans had become an all-but-universal outlet for a no-holds-barred conservatism, the Democrats the forum for an equally dominant liberalism. This has its virtues in intellectual thought but has also made policy swings after elections far wilder.

The dilemma for the party system has become something different. Within these ideological camps, the prospect of the party being captured by a charismatic and well-organised person and then reshaped in their image has become much more plausible and probable. It has happened (in a more subtle form admittedly) to the Democrats under Mr Obama and (much more overtly) to the Republicans with Mr Trump. The 'known known' for US politics over the next twenty to twenty-five years is that this sort of purloining of political parties is practical and possible. The 'known unknown' is whether it will happen again, who the successful insurgent who overthrows the party establishment might be, and the impact of all this on the policies advanced by the US. It is far harder, in this respect, to be a long-sighted watcher of American politics than that of Chinese politics.

Despite all this, American society and its economy continued as if the shifting tectonic plates of its political structure and party system did not exist throughout most of the first quarter of this century and have the capacity to do exactly the same again in the 2026–2049 period. This is not unique. For most of the post-1945 era Italy has been seen as plagued by political incoherence as prime ministers and governments came and went at speed. That has not stopped the north of that nation from being among the most prosperous places in all of Europe (although the south is a different story). The US may cope as well and without such a harsh geographical divide as in Italy.

What this survey should, I believe, lead to is one overall final and firm assessment.

The United States and China are not akin to Sparta and Athens the best part of 2,500 years ago. These were city states which existed in close proximity to one another. One, Sparta, had (usually two) ruling kings, a militaristic instinct, little time for economic development or for cultural diversity, and a highly stratified social structure with a vast number of slaves, and was the indisputable master of land warfare. The other, Athens, was something more similar to a democracy, much more individualistic, cheered the arts and prized oratory, was more attracted by the merits of trade, and relied on its supremacy at sea to ensure its security as a society. A case could be made, as Thucydides in effect did, that Ancient Greece was too small for both.

This is not the world that the US and China now occupy or are likely to occupy in 2026–2049. Ancestor worship is being taken much too far in comparing them to Sparta and to Athens. They are not even the equivalent of the rivalries (and wars) associated with France vs. Spain, Britain vs. France, France vs. Germany, Britain and France vs. Germany or even the US vs. the USSR. They are not near neighbours geographically or engaged in a zero-sum game in global politics. They are societies and economies on separate paths, not lined up to crash head-on unavoidably. There is no Thucydides Trap inviting conflict in 2026–2049.

Those who think about international affairs should look to an alternative acclaimed thinker of classical times, Aristotle, for their inspiration. Born twenty or so years after the naval Battle of Aegospotami (405 BCE) had settled the Peloponnesian War in Sparta's favour and just over fifteen years after the death of Thucydides, this exceptional intellectual, a figure hailed by some as the father of philosophy and others as a father of science (with both accolades being awarded in certain quarters), wields an influence in the realm of ideas that continues to this day.

He was, as the quotation at the start of this conclusion indicates, a deep sceptic about conflict with a strong preference for diplomacy. That must be our stance too. Although he noted, to translate him admittedly quite loosely, 'wishing to be friends is quick work, but friendship is a slow ripening fruit', this is a wholly viable strategy for the US and China. We must set aside the Thucydides Trap and embrace the Aristotle Answer.

INDEX